KT-480-258

THE NEW STRATEGISTS

Creating Leaders at All Levels

STEPHEN J. WALL
SHANNON RYE WALL

THE FREE PRESS

New York   London   Toronto   Sydney   Tokyo   Singapore

S 658.4012 WAL

Copyright © 1995 by Stephen J. Wall and Shannon Rye Wall

All rights reserved. No part of this book may be reproduced or transmitted in any form or by any means, electronic or mechanical, including photocopying, recording, or by any information storage and retrieval system, without permission in writing from the Publisher.

The Free Press
A Division of Simon & Schuster Inc.
1230 Avenue of the Americas
New York, N.Y. 10020

Printed in the United States of America

printing number

1 2 3 4 5 6 7 8 9 10

Text design by Carla Bolte

Library of Congress Cataloging-in-Publication Data

Wall, Stephen J.
     The new strategists : creating leaders at all levels / Stephen J. Wall,
  Shannon Rye Wall.
        p.   cm.
     ISBN 0-02-874058-0
     1. Strategic planning.   2. Leadership.   3. Employee empowerment.
  I. Wall, Shannon Rye.   II. Title.
  HD30.28.W335   1995
  658.4'012—dc20   95-24096
                                                                        CIP

For Alissa and Jack

CONTENTS

PREFACE

Once considered the province of senior management, strategy is becoming everyone's business. Over the last thirty-plus years many, many books have been published on the topics of strategy and leadership. To be honest, we thought a long time before deciding to add another title to the long and distinguished list by authors who have contributed so much to our collective understanding in these areas. But we came to believe that we could help people and organizations become even stronger and more effective by highlighting this trend among leading-edge organizations in a variety of industries.

If you wrestle with the following sorts of questions in your work life, this book will be of interest to you.

For executives, managers and human resource professionals:

- "How can we get everyone in the organization to understand and buy into our current strategies?"
- "We've got to become more flexible, responsive and market-focused—but how?"
- "We've told people that they're empowered. Why don't they act like it?"
- "How can we hold onto the professionals we've spent so much time and money training and developing?"
- "How can we ensure that we'll have the leaders this organization needs in the future?"

For leaders at all levels of their organizations or people who aspire to be leaders:

- "How can I have more say in what this company does and how we do it?"
- "Why can't those people at the top see what's really going on around here?"
- "How can I keep my customers satisfied when this company's policies work against me?"
- "What do I need to do to be successful in this organization, to keep my job, and to advance?"

Our purpose in writing this book is to examine a critical shift in how strategy is being made in organizations today. Using examples from leading companies in a variety of industries, we describe a realistic and practical approach to strategy that many companies are embracing, and we offer tips for how people in your organization can become more involved in the making of strategy. We examine common dilemmas that come along with such a change and provide examples of companies that have found ways to resolve those dilemmas.

We also identify the roles people throughout organizations are playing in the strategy process, including the roles of front-line people, managers, and corporate executives. We outline the skills leaders at all levels need to become true participants in the process. The appendixes include brief questionnaires you can use to assess how well you are currently performing in your strategic role, a detailed process teams can use to guide their strategic planning efforts, and suggestions for how new strategists can build their skills.

The information, tools, and examples presented in this book are based on extensive research and our experience consulting with more than two hundred corporations over the last ten years. The research includes:

- Interviews with more than one hundred executives, team members, and human resource professionals on their roles in the strategy-making process.
- Data collected over the last ten years on the leadership and management practices and influence skills used by more than four thousand

managers and professionals. Information was gathered through two feedback questionnaires, Compass and Matrix, which were developed by Dr. Gary Yukl of the State University of New York at Albany and Manus. Dr. Yukl has published numerous articles in professional journals outlining the rigorous development and validation of these surveys.

- Surveys of four hundred managers and human resource professionals on the use of cross-functional teams in their organizations (conducted in 1993 and 1994).
- Facilitation and documentation of more than 150 strategic plans for organizations in a variety of industries.

The most important reason that we wrote this book is our strong belief in the concept of "the business." Businesses and society have a fundamentally symbiotic relationship. Businesses, well run, can make a great contribution to the progress of a society overall; as a society, businesses help us progress. By providing leaders with the tools, concepts, and models they can use to help their businesses fulfill their fundamental purpose, our hope is that businesses will have an even more positive effect on the society in which we all live and work. Businesses and business leaders have been too much maligned and not enough appreciated by society at large. For that reason also, we invite you to read this book; it is full of inspiring examples of business leaders who have made a difference.

This book summarizes the thinking of some of the best business leaders at all levels of their organizations. We hope it is a practical and thought-provoking guide to a new way of thinking about strategy: who makes it, at what level, where, when, why, and how.

ACKNOWLEDGMENTS

Like strategy-making, writing a book is a collaborative art. We send our thanks to everyone who helped us convert our vision into a reality. In particular, we would like to thank:

- Our clients and the leaders and organizations profiled in this book. The ideas and principles outlined here grew out of your experiences and your learning.
- Rick Lepsinger and Toni Lucia, Managing Partners at Manus; our long-standing partnership and friendship are a continuing source of inspiration, insight, and delight.
- Bill Jockle, whose expertise and deep understanding of strategy are reflected in each chapter of this book.
- Jon Briscoe, an intelligent and conscientious colleague who conducted many of the interviews cited in this book.
- Our professional associates, all experts in their fields, who took the time to give us their recommendations and advice: Ray Bard, Jack Covert, Stan Davis, David DeVries, Jim Kouzes, Penny Nieroth, Len Sayles, Harold Scharlatt, Randy White, Richard Whiteley, and Gary Yukl.
- Our colleagues at Manus and our family and friends who offered their help, suggestions, and support throughout the process: Marc Berger, Marie Boccuzzi, Erik Campbell, Janet Castricum, Howard Cohen, Shay Dvoretzky, Debbie Horne, Ron Ignasiak, Jennifer Jordan, Al Keiser,

Blair Murray, Anna Ongpin, Dady Placide à François, Bernard Rosenbaum, Evelyn Toynton, Arch Turrentine, Jean Turrentine, Laurie Tubbs, Bonnie Uslianer, Martha Vinasco, David Wall, Thaddeus Ward, and Nanette Wright.

- Our associates and friends in the Instructional Systems Association, who gave us their words of wisdom and encouragement.
- Our editor at The Free Press, Robert Wallace, who believed in this project and continues to impress us with his extensive expertise and wisdom.
- Thanks, finally, to each of you who will take the time to read this book. We welcome your reactions and invite you to contact us with your input and suggestions. You can reach us at 203-326-3880. We look forward to hearing from you.

ABOUT THE AUTHORS

Stephen J. Wall is president of Manus, a U.S.-based consulting firm specializing in managing strategy and leading people. He designs and facilitates organizational change, strategic planning, and teambuilding sessions for strategy-making teams in a wide variety of industries. In addition to his consulting activities, Steve addresses conferences and leads workshops on strategic management and leadership at all levels. Recent clients include General Motors, The Tennessee Valley Authority, GE Capital, Canadian Imperial Bank of Commerce, Lehrer McGovern Bovis, Inter-Continental Hotels, and The Geon Company. He is the immediate past president of the Instructional Systems Association, a group of 150 top training and consulting firms. In his free time, Steve rides his BMW R1100-GS motorcycle in remote and beautiful locations.

Shannon Rye Wall is a senior consultant with Manus. She has developed and facilitated consulting interventions and training programs focusing on strategic leadership, management, and influence skills for Manus's clients, including Boston University's Leadership Institute, the Center for Creative Leadership, and The Prudential. Her work has included the documentation of over one hundred strategic business plans. Before joining Manus, Shannon taught writing at New York University; she is also a professional actress.

Steve and Shannon's long-term "joint venture" is their son, Jack Ryan Wall, born on Christmas Eve, 1993.

PART ONE

Strategy
What, Why, When, Where, and How?

1

Strategy

Myths, Misconceptions, and
Wrongheaded Notions

Ask yourself these questions:

1. In your company, who is responsible for creating the strategy?
2. If we were looking for your business' strategy, where would we find it?
3. Which comes first, the strategy or the tactics?
4. How do people come up with strategies?

When we ask people in business organizations those questions, these are their most frequent responses:

1. "The CEO comes up with the strategy. Well, the top team gives their input, but it's really the CEO." (Usually followed by a statement like: "And the CEO is retiring at the end of this year, so we won't really know what our strategies are for a while. Things are kind of on hold.")
2. "Our strategy? Oh, it's right here in this binder."
3. "First you plan the strategy—then you decide on the tactics to carry it out."
4. "Gee, I think the right strategies just kind of come to you, you know,

3

in the shower, or when you're running . . . you just have a moment of inspiration."

If similar ideas about strategy can be heard around the halls and cubicles of your organization—or if you found yourself nodding in agreement as you read the above remarks—you're about to be left behind. Why? Because progressive organizations in many industries are developing a new approach to strategy—an approach that is likely to give them a competitive advantage in the coming years.

Let's look at the most common misconceptions about strategy and, in the process, explain why the new view of strategy is so critical to your organization's future.

MISCONCEPTION 1: STRATEGY? THAT'S THE CEO'S JOB.

This is probably the most widespread misconception: it's the CEO's job to come up with the strategies. (A variant is the idea that "top management" makes the strategy, with "top" defined as those at least two levels above the person using the term.)

The press doesn't help. Business publications frequently report on company strategies by invoking the name of the CEO and describing the strategies he or she is currently pursuing. The implication is that a lone leader comes up with the company's strategies in isolation, without input from others in the organization. The success or failure of the strategies is also laid at the feet of the leader—rarely at those of even the top management team.

Consider these magazine headlines from the past few years:

- "*Andy Grove—How Intel Makes Spending Pay Off*: Intel's CEO bet billions on R&D and new plants"
- "*Steve Jobs' Next Big Gamble*: The legendary entrepreneur aims to survive by transforming the hardware maker into a major player in software that runs on other companies' computers"
- "*Can Larry Beat Bill?*: Oracle CEO Larry Ellison's goal: To conquer Microsoft on the I-way"

- "*Gault on Fixing Goodyear's Flat:* Stan Gault put bounce into Rubbermaid and became a business superstar. Now, as chief executive of his troubled Ohio neighbor, he tells how he'll tackle his greatest challenge yet"
- "*Can Lou Gerstner Save IBM?:* He may not know computers from crackers, but the new Big Man at Big Blue, Lou Gerstner, knows how to shake up and rebuild corporate cultures" (followed some time later by: *Is He Too Cautious to Save IBM?*)

While the leader of an organization may bear final responsibility for selecting the overall strategic direction of the enterprise, the leader can hardly be expected to formulate (and can certainly not implement) strategies singlehanded.

What's most intriguing is that our deification of the leader exists side by side with a cry for more participatory organizations, a deemphasis of hierarchy, and a renewed focus on teamwork. While decisions about daily operations and incremental improvements are being pushed further down in the organization, more often than not the creation of strategy is still seen as the province of the CEO. This insistence on anointing the leader as the one solely responsible for determining strategic direction is a curious throwback to the paternalistic mindset so many companies are trying to leave behind.

The depiction of the CEO as lone ranger may be related to the conception of top executives as military generals. As many writers have noted, the concept of business strategy has its roots in military leadership. The word "strategy" is derived from two Greek words: "stratos," meaning an army, and "legein," meaning to lead. While leading an organization and leading an army do have something in common (inspiring "the troops," seeing the big picture, marshaling resources), business is not war.

Although there are useful lessons to be learned from examining military history, thinking of strategy in this way can also be misleading. Employees are not foot soldiers who obey commands. Generals derive their power from an actual or anticipated crisis; for the good of the whole, the army accepts leadership by edict. While many organizations are trying to abandon such command-and-control mentality, perceptions of strategy are still mired in its military roots. We need to lay aside our view of business strategy as something conceived in the mind of the brilliant general and carried out by soldiers, and learn to see it in a way that involves tapping the strategic thinking skills of leaders at all levels of the organization.

(Interestingly enough, military organizations themselves are changing the way they develop strategies, at least according to Compton's Encyclopedia: "Modern warfare has permanently altered the nature of strategy. One general alone no longer plans wars, campaigns or battles . . . Many planning functions must be delegated. Strategy creation now more resembles the planning sessions of a major corporation.")

For an example of how leaders emerged from relatively low levels of an organization to transform their business's strategy, consider Cincinnati Milacron. In 1985 this maker of plastics injection-molding machines was routinely being beaten by superior foreign imports that had managed to seize over 50 percent of the U.S. market in just under ten years. Harold Faig, a product manager, and Bruce Kozak, a young salesman, were tired of losing sales to Nissei and Toshiba. One Sunday over coffee they began listing the specifications that a machine would need to beat the Japanese. Faig, now a group vice president, describes the strategy that emerged from their discussion:

> There was no question about the technology of our machines, the quality and reliability . . . it was simply a matter of providing a product to the market with lower cost and better features. The strategy that evolved, very simply then, was to completely focus on the Japanese and to go after the market with as much intensity and focus as we could.*

Faig approached his boss with their idea for a new machine that could win against the company's foreign competitors: "When I went in with the program, I made it very clear to my boss: 'Look, if you're not in a position to defend this and keep the wolves away, it will never happen.'"

---

*All quotations not attributed to published sources are drawn from personal interviews. They are reproduced with the permission of those interviewed.

To his surprise, he and Kozak got the go-ahead. He assembled a cross-functional team that developed the dream machine in nine months—less than half the usual development time. In their first year of production the new Vista machine sold nearly three times as well as its predecessor. By combining their knowledge of what customers wanted with their drive to influence the company's future, the two front-line strategists came up with a breakthrough product that saved the organization. Cincinnati Milacron is the only surviving major U.S. producer of this type of injection-molding machine. In 1994 *Industry Week* cited their Batavia, Ohio manufacturing operation as one of the top ten plants in the United States.

Looking back on the project nine years later, Faig describes his philosophy:

> I had a personal feeling that it wasn't senior management's responsibility to come up with direction on what we were going to do—that belonged down in the bowels of the organization. If we are all doing our job, we're going to them and saying "Hey, here's where we need to go." Then, management's responsibility is to say, "Does that fit into the strategies and direction that we're really looking for?"

Another great example of the new breed of strategist comes from Thermo Electron's San Diego labs. Thermo Electron is an extremely successful company with a wide variety of separate businesses. It makes products for instrumentation, biomedical, and other high-tech applications.

One of the most innovative new products—a laser-based hair-removal process—is the brainchild of a Russian scientist, a recent emigré employed by the company's ThermoTrex subsidiary. After accidentally zapping himself on the leg with a laser, he noticed that the hair fell out in the spot he had zapped. A specialist in laser technology, the scientist thought, "Maybe I've stumbled across a technology to remove hair."

According to the CEO, George Hatsopoulos, the subsidiary president, Ken Tang, was less than enthusiastic when he heard about the potential new business. "Imagine Thermo Electron, with all our high technology, going into the hair-removal business. It seemed ridiculous." But the scientist was so persistent, and an analysis of the market was so promising, that Ken decided to take a chance and suggest to Thermo Electron's Operating Committee that they consider entering the market. Hatsopoulos described what happened next:

> They took a lot of abuse by even bringing the idea up. But the more we thought about it, we found out that this was a one billion dollar market in the U.S. The hair-removal process of electrolysis is very painful, very expensive and not very effective. So we decided to go into that business. Now we have a spinout called Thermolase, which is developing that technology.

Thermolase got FDA approval in 1995. In the first five months of that year, share price climbed 280 percent. "Things like this have happened many times," notes Hatsopoulos. "Most of the ideas for our new businesses did not come from the top of the organization."

In most companies, however, people below the senior level don't see strategy-making as part of their jobs. Think of your own company. How many times have you heard people say, "Well, we don't really know where we're going (and we can't make a decision on this) until *they* tell us what the strategy is"?

As consultants to a broad spectrum of companies, we frequently see such reluctance to take responsibility for strategy in our management development programs. During these workshops, managers take part in a simulation. They assume the roles of the top twenty executives of a fictitious corporation. After reviewing memos on the industry, the company, and its strategy to date, one brave manager will take the role of CEO, while others become the presidents and vice presidents of the various divisions. They have complete freedom to run the company as they see fit, taking actions and making decisions about the company's future.

Now, these are generally senior managers or high-potential middle managers in large corporations. They are colleagues in real life, often on the same level, with similar backgrounds. Over and over again, we've seen people at the vice president level sit at their desks and wait for the presidents and the CEO to tell them what the strategies are before taking any action or offering any recommendation. In one group, the Management Committee took four hours to come back to the vice presidents with its statement of strategic direction. Meanwhile, those managers, each with more than fifty memos at hand outlining issues and possible strategies for the organization, *waited* for direction. We'd like to think that this happens only in simulations, but we believe that real life has taught these executives that their role is only to *implement* strategies, not to make them.

For the sake of argument, let's say that the role of people at lower levels of the organization *is* to implement, rather than to formulate, strategies. Isn't this still a meaningful contribution to the strategy process? It can be. However, playing a significant role in strategy implementation requires that the implementers actually understand what the company's strategy is. Such understanding turns out to be the exception rather than the rule. A recent study by the Council of Communication Management found that 61 percent of employees surveyed said they aren't well informed about company plans.[1]

The perceived lack of direction from the top can result in lack of co-ordination, confusion, and wasted time. Seen from another perspective, however, it provides opportunities for leaders at all levels to make strategic decisions without undue interference.

Edward Wrapp, management theorist, puts it this way:

> Subordinates who keep pressing for more precise objectives are in truth working against their own best interests. Each time the objectives are stated more specifically, a subordinate's range of possibilities for operating is reduced. The narrower field means less room to roam and to accommodate the flow of ideas coming up from his part of the organization.[2]

The problem, then, is not just that management fails to communicate its strategic intentions to the rest of the organization. The problem is that the rest of the organization has come to think of the CEO and other top managers as the sole strategy-makers. What we need are leaders throughout the organization who are adept strategic thinkers, that is, people who understand the connection between their daily actions and the business's strategy, and who have the drive and skills to get their ideas heard and implemented.

Why is it so important that people throughout the organization see themselves as strategists? The answer is this: Wherever you are in the organization, whether you're a member of a project team, or a manager, or a corporate executive, you are already part of the strategy process. Your actions can propel or derail the success of the current strategies. Your actions can also be the basis for the evolution of entirely new strategies.

Actions developing into strategies? Before we go too much further, let us clarify what we mean by strategy in the first place. We'll do so by examining another misconception.

MISCONCEPTION 2: STRATEGY? IT'S IN THE BINDER.

When we ask people for their definitions of strategy, they often emphasize the planned, deliberate, and programmed process which has come to be associated with strategic planning. "Strategy is a plan of action," or "Strategy is the overall direction of the company as set by the top management," or "Strategy is how you plan to get where you want to go." An executive put it this way: "If you ask people in this organization for our strategy, they'll haul in three big binders."

Many management theorists who debate such things for a living stress this same formal, deliberate nature of strategy:

- "At its simplest, a strategy can be a very specific plan of action directed at a specified result within a specific period of time."[3]
- "[Strategy is] the adoption of courses of action and the allocation of resources necessary for carrying out these goals."[4]
- "In everyday parlance, strategy is a plan for getting things done."[5]

While it would be hard to argue that those definitions are wrong, they only tell half the story of how strategies actually come about. There is a growing awareness among many who study organizations that strategy involves much more than the plan that's put in the binder that's put on the shelf.

Robert Eccles and Nitin Nohria see it this way:

Strategy is not merely something that is *devised;* it is also something that *happens*—it emerges constantly in a firm as different people respond to and reinterpret their sense of the organization's identity and purpose.[6]

Strategy, then, is like the plot of a novel. If you were writing a novel, how would you develop the plot? Well, you could start with a very detailed outline and know before you wrote the first sentence exactly where you wanted the story to go. Or you could start with only a central image, event or character and let the story emerge as you wrote it. It is most likely that you'd use some combination of the two approaches: Start with some plan and then be flexible enough to modify it as you go. However you arrive at it, your completed novel will have a plot. However it is created, your business has a strategy. And the plan formulated in advance is only part of it.

In other words, strategy does not just involve *planning;* it also involves *doing.* And sometimes the doing actually comes before the planning. This view of strategy flies in the face of the linear process we all learned in school: Plan, then act. While this sequence may be logical, in reality we often act and then use the results of our actions to decide on the next step.

For this reason, we prefer the term "strategy-making" to phrases like "strategic planning," or "strategizing," which emphasize the formal process by which strategies are developed but ignore the fact that strategies often evolve through action.

Now, unlike some of those who study management, we're not advocating that you throw the strategic planning baby out with the bath water. Your organization needs the sense of focus and direction provided by a formal plan. But strategies must also be allowed to evolve in response to changes in the environment, and plans need to be modified accordingly. Sometimes the most useful thing about plans is that they remind you what you're deviating from.

Formal strategic plans come from an assessment of current conditions and your predictions of what will happen in the future. Because this evaluation may be based on incomplete information or inadequate analysis, and because the environment is dynamic and unpredictable, recognizing strategies as they evolve can be critical to your organization's success.

Particularly when you're entering a new or quickly changing market, it is critical to allow strategies to evolve. When IBM's Research Division decided to focus on the still emerging multimedia market, it realized that IBM had to go after this market "niche by niche, not with a grand scheme."[7] Does that mean IBM lacks a strategy for the multimedia market? To the contrary, they are letting the strategy evolve through the discovery of what works and what doesn't.

Vice President Mark Bregman, who is responsible for the Research Division's strategy in the areas of Physical Sciences and Technology, puts it this way:

> I don't think it's clear at this point exactly what the multimedia market is. I recently went to a meeting that included people from television, cable, production and telecommunications companies. Everyone who spoke described how they saw the future of the multimedia industry—and everyone had a different future, with their company at the center of it. At this point, we don't have a monolithic strategy for this market—and it would be inappropriate if we did.

Why is this difference in how strategy is defined so important to your business? It may not be, if you are in a stable industry, if your markets and customers want the same thing year after year, if your competitors are asleep or nonexistent. Fewer and fewer businesses, however, find themselves in that fortunate position. When the International Consortium for Executive Development Research recently surveyed more than 1,200 executives worldwide, they found that the respondents viewed "being flexible to meet new competitive conditions" as one of the top five organizational capabilities in need of development.[8]

Flexibility is possible only if your strategies are allowed to evolve, as well as being formally planned. In essence, you need to plan for flexibility, to develop ways to encourage evolving strategies to percolate through your organization. People at all levels need to be encouraged not only to carry out strategies but to respond to them, to initiate them, and to adapt them to new circumstances. The "first plan, then act" mindset is deeply ingrained. It's going to take your initiative and leadership to change it.

MISCONCEPTION 3: FIRST YOU PLAN THE STRATEGY, THEN YOU DECIDE ON THE TACTICS TO CARRY IT OUT.

The increased need for flexibility requires another shift in how you view strategy. The very nature of evolutionary strategy-making is to allow today's actions to become tomorrow's strategies. And we're not just talking about the actions of the CEO or management team. In the process of implementation, strategies are continually reshaped, as people in every job respond to customers, sign up new clients, work with suppliers, design new products, and refine existing ones. Teams and individuals who are making decisions and taking action to respond to and anticipate customer needs are, in fact, making important contributions to the actual strategy of your business.

Some might argue decisions of that sort fall under the category of *tactics* rather than *strategy*. In the traditional approach to strategic planning, tactics were seen as means for arriving at the end decided on by senior management, and therefore the province of the "detail" people several levels down.

However, in conditions of rapid change, the distinction between strategy and tactics is simply not useful any more. The management expert Henry Mintzberg makes this argument quite clearly:

> Decisions made for immediate purposes under short-run pressures— whether to handle a crisis or seize an opportunity—can have the most long-range and strategic of consequences. . . . Likewise, seemingly momentous "strategic" decisions can sometimes fizzle like a punctured balloon. The trouble with the strategy–tactics distinction is that one can never be sure which is which until all the dust has settled.[9]

Because formulation and implementation of strategy cannot be separated clearly, and because the rapid pace of change requires frequent adaptation of strategies that have been set, today's tactic may become the basis of tomorrow's strategy.

For an example, let's go back to IBM's Research Division. As long as their project goals are met, researchers in the division are free to spend their time on projects of their choice. In 1993 several separate researchers became interested in using information technology to improve education in grades K–12. Unknown to each other, they began working on the initial, unfunded stages of those different projects. Some went out and met with people in the schools to get a clearer picture of their needs.

Once a year researchers submit project descriptions, which outline the work they are doing; those documents are used to motivate allocation of resources to projects during the division's planning process. Upon reviewing the project descriptions, senior management discovered that there were several projects under way in the area of education. That prompted them to develop an R&D strategy for the K–12 education market, a strategy that focused and integrated the work being done in the division.

That strategy would never have emerged had the researchers involved seen their role as the implementation of tactics in support of the division's existing strategies. In this case, the tactics actually preceded and drove the strategy. Do individuals and teams in your organization have the power, the drive, and the skills to identify and create new strategies? Does your organization convert successful tactics into formal strategies? If it doesn't, your company may be overlooking a major opportunity to gain a lasting and resilient competitive advantage.

MISCONCEPTION 4: STRATEGY? IT COMES TO YOU IN THE SHOWER.

How do strategies come about? We tend to think that strategies are born in the minds of individuals, especially individuals at the top of the organization. Even in the rare cases when strategy-making is recognized as occurring at other levels of the organization, it is virtually always attributed to a single, brilliant manager who had a vision and persuaded higher-ups to support it.[10]

In many organizations, however, strategy is increasingly being made by teams rather than individuals. Strategies are created at a round table, on a flip chart, in the field talking with customers, not just in the shower. They are born from the combined experiences and conversations of many minds.

Peter Vaill, a management writer, noted that people with a "knack for strategic planning realize that strategic thinking can no longer be the solitary enterprise of one wise person, that it cannot be done in a closet or on a mountain top, but rather that it is a social, interactive process in which the task is to learn to use the diverse talents and experiences that there are available in the organization."[11]

Why is the creation of strategy shifting from individuals to teams? As proponents of a team culture point out, no individual has as much information, influence, or analytical smarts as a well-functioning group of people does. And, even if he or she *did,* other people would still be needed to carry out the strategy (thus modifying and shaping it along the way).

The reason why "two heads are better than one" is not just that two people can generate more ideas than one can. Teams of people with diverse styles can overcome the limitations of any single person's style. Your work style is not simply a matter of easily learnable skills but is, in fact, a deeply rooted preference linked to your basic character or personality. Though you can to some extent change your behavior consciously, your preferred style comes most naturally. Style determines not only where you are inclined to focus but also what you typically fail to attend to. It acts as a kind of screen, limiting the input you receive and how you make sense of it.[12]

You also choose to attend to and screen out information based on your role in the organization. In order to cope with the range of issues and mass of data in the organization, you have to filter out the less critical input. A marketing manager is most likely to pay attention to feedback that is most useful for marketing efforts; an R&D scientist will probably focus on different kinds of issues and information.

A vice president at Northern Telecom describes why his corporation decided to bring together people from each business unit and function in what they call their Global Leadership Forum. That effort has two overall goals: to develop each leader's skills and to solve real business problems. "We wanted to bring the widest diversity of ideas to each team so we could stimulate breakthrough thinking. If we are working on a manufacturing problem and we just use manufacturing people, the solution won't be nearly as good as it could be," he says.

A team of individuals, all with different styles, job responsibilities, backgrounds and experiences, can pay attention to a wider range of information, feedback, and input from customers and markets. For this reason, teams, rather than individuals, are becoming the primary unit responsible for the development and implementation of strategy.

The late 1980s and early 1990s have seen a headlong rush toward team-based organizations. As we write this, several best-selling business books focus on how to get teams to function effectively. In the desire to understand how teams work and what makes them successful, people too often jump to a discussion of the team process: how people work together, how they communicate, how to hold teams accountable, how to reward and encourage teamwork. What is left out is the context: *why* teams are being encouraged.

Teams should be used because they offer a better way to implement a particular strategy. A cross-functional team reengineering a business process should be doing so in pursuit of a specific strategy—perhaps creating efficiencies in order to maintain market share, perhaps streamlining in order to remain competitive in an all-out market war with a key competitor. And in the implementation of those strategies, teams of people are *making* strategy as well.

The very nature of teamwork encourages the evolution of strategy. As people work together, bouncing ideas off each other, they tend to refine and develop them as they converse. In the course of their work, they may discover customer needs that have previously gone unnoticed. As they take action to address those needs, and as those actions meet with success, strategies quietly but surely emerge—strategies that are grounded in the realities of customer expectations and conditions in the market environment.

Since they are likely to be key players in the strategy process, team members need to be well versed in the formal strategies your business is pursuing. For example, if you are a member of a marketing team coming up with a new promotional effort, and you understand that you need to support a market penetration strategy, you will choose quite different tactics from those required if the strategy were to maintain market share. Members of a product development team need to understand the ins and outs of the current competitive climate before they can make useful decisions about what features will really give the new product an advantage.

And the strategies themselves must be flexible enough to change if the team uncovers new information about shifts in the marketplace. Team members need to see themselves as front-line strategists, rather than foot soldiers expected to play a preordained role in pursuit of inflexible goals handed down from the top of the organization. In fact, the more people in your company, regardless of their level, who see themselves as strategists, the more likely you are to have a strong, resilient organization that is in tune with its environment.

IN SUMMARY . . .

Strategy is a dynamic process incorporating much more than the deliberate, linear sequence that has come to be associated with strategic planning. Our model (see next page) depicts how strategies are actually created and what the specific elements are of the dynamic process we call strategy-making.[13] It reconciles two of the key debates, or false dichotomies, that have been swirling around the subject of strategy over the last twenty years: Are strategies formulated via a deliberate, formal process, or do they emerge unplanned? (Both are true.) And does strategy entail finding a fit between your current capabilities and the marketplace, or does it involve anticipating as yet unseen trends and thus transforming the company and even the industry? (It entails both.)

This process has no distinct beginning, middle, or end. Leaders who are managing strategy can begin at any of the four points depicted in the figure. The sequence of events is less critical than being sure to recognize and manage all four aspects of strategy-making.

For the sake of this description, we'll start at the top of the circle: *Deliberate strategies* are developed based on detailed analyses of the indus-

Strategy: A Dynamic Learning Process

In turn,
Deliberate Strategies are
developed and
revised...

...**Strategic Foresight** based
on discovering unanticipated
markets and unarticulated
customer needs...

...and tested for
their **Strategic Fit**
with customers
and markets...

New strategies also
Evolve based on
the learnings of
front-line strategists,
leading to...

try environment and the business's competitive position within it. This is the formal process known as "strategic planning," which involves focusing the organization on key strategies and on allocating resources according to the plan.

Even the most carefully formulated plans, however, change and evolve as they are tested for their *strategic fit* with customers and markets. After all, a strategic plan is really based on a business's best predictions of the future. These predictions are tested and revised based on feedback from customers and new information about developments in the market environment. Competitors' moves also affect the viability of the formal plans.

Out of this testing process, new *strategies evolve* based on the acquired knowledge of a new kind of strategist, the front-line employee.

As employees interact with customers and invent new ways of responding to customers' needs, they develop new strategic approaches that can then evolve into more formal strategies.

When strategic leaders capitalize on the wealth of information and knowledge that is accumulated by front-line strategists, they develop *strategic foresight*—the ability to discover unanticipated market trends and as yet unarticulated customer needs. Businesses with strategic foresight avoid the trap of developing strategies that are merely reactive, and are able to discover possibilities that may ultimately transform their companies and their industries.

Based on the strategic fit of the strategies that are currently being tested, new strategies that are evolving, and new possibilities that are being uncovered, *deliberate strategies* are revised and new strategies are formulated.

In the next chapter, we'll explain more about why strategy is everyone's business and discuss some of the benefits to getting your entire organization involved in the strategy-making process.

2

Beyond the Boardroom
Why Strategy Is Everyone's Business

Power in the system was concentrated at the top. Only top managers, the gospel went, had enough information to make decisions. . . . The system disenfranchised those who were so important in the early stages of American manufacturing, the foremen and plant managers. Instead of being creators and innovators, as in an earlier era, now they depended on meeting production quotas. They lost any stake in stopping the line and fixing problems as they occurred; they lost any stake in innovation or change.
—Robert McNamara[1]

Why is it so important that strategy become everyone's business in your organization? What was wrong with the old way, when top management went off to the woods for a few days each year, reviewed competing proposals from the various businesses, came up with the formal strategy, and let everyone else know what it was?

This kind of top-down, once-a-year process of codifying strategies may have worked well (though it often didn't) when the environment was calmer, when you sold the same products to basically the same people every year, when life was more predictable. It was assumed, not always wrongly, that important changes in the marketplace would become apparent to top management in time to be incorporated into the next plan;

21

customer loyalty and a generally moderate level of competition ensured that there would be time to adapt before any damage was done to the organization's competitiveness. If the ongoing process of correcting for mistakes was slow, so were the shifts in the marketplace itself.

Now that kind of environmental stability has mostly vanished, and in its wake has come a terrifically competitive, volatile global marketplace in which the time frames for responding to changing customer needs have been radically shortened. In a 1994 study, Battelle Memorial Institute found that "companies are pushing products to the market more quickly. And new products have a shorter economic life before being displaced by newer designs."[2]

Businesses today are facing a broad array of new challenges, and those challenges require a new approach. They are turning to wider participation in strategy-making to help them achieve an advantage over their competitors in a rapidly changing market arena. This broader input is paying off, according to a research study conducted by Gordon Group, Inc., for the California Public Employees' Retirement System (CalPERS). This study found that "companies that involve employees more often in decision-making boast stronger market valuations than those that don't."[3]

Getting more people involved in strategy-making can help your organization meet these kinds of challenges:

- Focusing on your customers and markets
- Staying flexible and responsive
- Holding onto valuable, knowledgeable employees
- Avoiding management burnout

FOCUSING ON YOUR CUSTOMERS AND MARKETS

In rapidly changing competitive conditions, information about what customers need, what competitors can do, and how your company's products and services stack up is critical. People who are closest to the customer on a daily basis (and that's not normally top management) often have the best data. In many organizations, critical information never makes it to the strategists at the top. As the economist Kenneth Boulding said, "The very purpose of a hierarchy is to prevent information from reaching higher layers. It operates as an information filter, and there are little wastebaskets all along the way."[4]

When 3M's Occupational Health and Environmental Safety Division conducted an internal study in the mid-1980s, it found that 50 percent of middle management's time was devoted to filtering information up and down the organization. When the division revamped its product development process and gave cross-functional development teams a direct pipeline to the top management team or operating committee, division leaders found that "the information flow improved exponentially between the teams and the Operating Committee, both of them getting far more information than they would have gotten before."

Even when information does reach the senior levels, it is often ignored or denied. Large U.S. corporations, from auto makers to high-tech companies, have been faulted for failing to spot emerging trends that indicate the need for a major shift in strategic direction. Senior executives, in particular, may be most insulated from information that could mean bad news, and most attached to ways of operating that have been successful in the past. The psychologist Harry Levinson describes this phenomenon:

> The more successful one becomes, the higher one's occupational self-esteem. The higher one rises in an organization, the more self-confidence one is likely to develop about one's proficiency and one's roles. Concomitantly, the higher one rises, the less supervision one is likely to have. The combination of these factors frequently gives rise to . . . overconfidence and a sense of entitlement. That, in turn, leads to denial of those realities that threaten the inflated self-image and to contempt for other individuals and organizations. It also leads to less tolerance for deviations from the already successful model.[5]

By making people at all levels responsible for strategy-making, you can counter the tendency toward top management myopia and open up the eyes and ears of your organization. That encourages a focus on the market and on relevant data, good or bad.

The team that developed GM's successful Aurora car provides a great example of how a focus on the customer changed the way things were done at Oldsmobile. In 1992 a former GM car owner remarked, "They need to ask people, 'How do you like that car?' I bet not one in ten of them has done that."[6] Oldsmobile did. Douglas Stott, Aurora Project Line Engineering Manager, describes the process they used to create the Aurora, which was named a 1994 Product of the Year by both *Fortune* and *Business Week:*

> We really started this project doing what we call the "voice of the customer." In other words, we went out and talked to people about what their next car should be like, rather than trying to decide ourselves and then saying "Don't you like it?"
>
> The focus groups were very straightforward in their answers. "If you put 'Oldsmobile' on it, the first thing everybody is going to think is 'Well, it's just an Oldsmobile.' No matter how good it is, it won't be evaluated on its true merits. . . . The way to do it is to do a car that's right and to put some new name on it." So that's what we did! We took the rockets off, people started evaluating the car on its own merits, and the car became a real winner.
>
> We've proven that if you listen to the people, do what they say, and hold to your guns, in spite of what those about you are saying, you can win.

At Becton Dickinson, a New Jersey manufacturer of high-tech medical equipment, eight strategic planning teams are responsible for continuously setting and implementing strategies for their divisions. Chuck Baer, President of the Consumer Products Division, is a member of his unit's planning team; so are representatives from various functions and locations throughout the world. The team meets twice a year in person and much more frequently via conference calls.

Becton Dickinson's managers learned from experience that, in order to be a truly worldwide competitor, they had to get more people involved in strategy-making. "The early strategies," Baer says, "were primarily U.S. based, and, for the most part, very little input from outside the U.S. was considered. But some of the developments were taking place outside the U.S., and they didn't find their way into our strategies.

We were also not able to develop strategy that might meet the needs that were different than the needs of the people in the U.S."

Now that people from around the world are part of the strategy process, Baer says, "what we believe is that by sensing what's going on around the world, we're not going to get blindsided by anybody who might be creating something in one part of the world but not another. And if we find some development from R&D and some manufacturing opportunities, then we can immediately pull a team together and decide what we want to do. This enables us not only to take advantage of something we develop, but to react quickly to any threat we might see."

STAYING FLEXIBLE AND RESPONSIVE

As Chuck Baer suggests, it's not enough merely to focus on your customers and markets. Such a focus will provide a competitive advantage only if your organization's plans are flexible enough to accommodate the new information you gather.

While you may start out with a deliberate plan, it's bound to change as you begin to carry it out. Because the future is so hard to predict, unforeseen events rear their ugly or at times beneficent heads. The plan changes in reaction to those events, or as you see what works and what doesn't. If leaders throughout the organization see their role as merely the carrying out of a plan handed down from on high, they aren't as likely to adapt the strategy to new circumstances. If, on the other hand, they see themselves as strategy-makers with the power to shape the strategies as necessary, they are likely to act more flexibly and responsively.

At The Geon Company, a new company formed from a division of B. F. Goodrich, a desire to become more flexible and responsive led to a complete overhaul of the strategic planning process. Geon is one of North America's largest producers of PVC resin and PVC-based compounds for construction and automotive uses. Geon's customers were demanding more timely responses to their needs, which the company's functional organization and history of being driven by internal processes made very difficult at first. To correct the situation, senior managers, who had determined that the overall strategic direction for the company should be a more focused penetration of certain markets, established cross-functional business teams to achieve this broad mandate.

Those teams set about planning for product development: determining which new products were necessary to compete successfully in target markets, which existing products were most profitable, and which gave the company a distinct advantage with customers. To do so, they gathered and analyzed input from customers and from people in various parts of the organization.

For the first time in its history, Geon was determining what products it should manufacture and what modifications should be made based on customers' descriptions of their needs rather than on internal factors. The question was no longer, "Can we sell Cadillac on this new type of resin our design people have come up with?" but rather, "What kind of resin should we be developing, given what Cadillac needs for next year?"

Once the business teams had arrived at their determinations, responsibility for allocating resources and overseeing operations was given to market segment teams. But the market segment teams were not simply engaged in carrying out the strategy that had been formulated at higher levels. "We now make decisions standing at the coffee-maker that used to be made by the Senior Management Committee," reports Glenn Higby, Geon's Director of Manufacturing. The team members' hands-on understanding of processes, products, and markets resulted in a number of modifications and even led to the reversal of certain decisions made by more senior people.

For example, a plant that had been scheduled for closure within a few weeks of the time the planning teams met was saved from the ax when team members from R&D and Marketing pointed out that a product that could be made at that plant alone—and which Manufacturing had judged equivalent to another product made elsewhere—was not at all equivalent in the eyes of the customer.

In another case, the people in Manufacturing had decided to shift the manufacture of a particular product from one site to another in order to achieve greater production efficiencies. Team members from Distribution and Sales, however, recognized that increased distribution and delivery costs to customers in other regions of the country would actually make for an increase in overall costs. The plan was changed.

The new planning structure enabled decisions to be made more flexibly on line, without the team members having to seek approval from dozens of people. At the same time, the cross-functional character of the teams ensured that decisions would be made with the input of a variety of functions and businesses.

By redesigning its strategy-making process to emphasize wider participation, Geon achieved the flexibility and responsiveness that have proved key to its successful turnaround. In 1992, when still part of B. F. Goodrich, Geon lost $27 million. In the period between April 1993 and March 1994, it posted $31.8 million in operating income. *Forbes* magazine called it "a splendid example of how a producer of a commodity product can be run profitably."[7]

HOLDING ONTO VALUABLE, KNOWLEDGEABLE EMPLOYEES

Much has been written about the new breed of employees who want more control over their work lives and more say in how their companies operate. The cry for empowerment is aimed at tapping the skills of these (and all) people in the organization. However, empowerment is likely to be seen as hollow if employees feel powerless to affect the strategies the company is pursuing. And retaining those highly skilled and trained professionals will become increasingly important as knowledge has more and more to do with the company's ability to build and maintain a competitive advantage. Especially in businesses that rely on the provision of professional services, the only way to gain a competitive advantage is to have superior people—to be the employer of choice.

Leading-edge companies in a variety of industries are recognizing that "intellectual capital" is one of their most valuable assets. James Brian Quinn of the Tuck School of Business at Dartmouth estimates that, even in manufacturing, three-fourths of value added comes from the knowledge of the people in the business.[8] Organizations like Dow Chemical, Skandia, Hughes Aircraft and the Canadian Imperial Bank of

Commerce are working hard to find ways to measure and track their intellectual capital.

While this intellectual capital can be found in such tangible assets as the number of patents held by a company, it often resides in the heads of the people who do the work throughout the business. Despite Dorothy Parker's assertion that the "movie business is the only business in the world where the assets go home at night,"[9] companies in many other industries are paying more attention to the assets that can walk out the door.

If knowledge is truly to be a distinguishing characteristic of successful companies in the 1990s and beyond, companies will need to find a way to tap that knowledge and retain those skilled workers by giving them a stronger sense of purpose and control over their destinies. Theodore Levitt, a management writer, puts it this way:

> The more dependent the work of an organization is on the work of its professional knowledge workers (which include its managers), the more the organization must attend to their getting the professional and personal satisfactions that keep them inspired and in place. Whether they will depart to other places is only partly a matter of demand on the outside. Whether and how well they perform is almost entirely a matter of conditions on the inside.[10]

More and more organizations are making concerted efforts to improve employee retention. They are doing so by giving people more, not less, responsibility. Bob Price, who manages two 7-Eleven stores in The Colony, Texas, has restructured the jobs of store clerks, giving them responsibility for specific areas of the stores. Whereas they once saw their jobs as stocking shelves, cleaning, and running the register, clerks are now making decisions about what products to keep or discontinue, and how many to order based on detailed sales data that they generate. Price reports impressive results from this approach:

> The average tenure of my employees is over four years. For our industry, the average for the clerk position is 30–60 days. My personal feeling is that if you can get that employee committed and feeling that they are real-

ly making some decisions, they are going to feel a lot better about their position, and the longer they are going to stay with the company.

The Mount Bachelor Ski and Summer Resort credits its team-based planning process, which involves employees throughout the organization, with giving it a higher retention rate than industry averages. Ann Smith, VP of Human Resources, described the rationale behind its high-involvement culture:

> If you look at today's society and the people living in it and making things work, you no longer have the option of being a paternalistic or autocratic kind of business if you want to stay in business. Employee involvement in planning makes good business sense because people need to buy into what's going on—they need to own it in order to make it work.

Relatively progressive organizations have long recognized that the success of their strategic planning processes depends on a sense of ownership among those who would actually be carrying out the plan. However, it was too often seen as sufficient to make rather token gestures of accommodation. Meetings may have been held after the fact in order to enlist the commitment and cooperation of lower-level managers, but the emphasis was on "communicating" the strategy (telling people what it was), instead of allowing people to influence it.

This one-way approach to communication is perpetuated by some who give advice to managers and leaders. One writer on strategic planning exhorted: "In order for planning to work, the entire management organization must feel itself part of the effort. There are too many closed-door, top-level meetings that are never summarized for the masses once meaningful direction has emerged."[11]

In order for people truly to understand and be committed to a strategy, we need to go beyond summaries for the masses and actually make people at all levels a part of the process. Businesses are beginning to recognize that they need fewer speeches and more dialogues—fewer final decisions and more working drafts asking for input and opinions.

Indeed, the plan document, which was once seen as a final outcome, carved in stone, may now be regarded as merely a starting point for discussion. In some progressive organizations, it is not intended to be accepted as a given but instead to have holes poked in it, to be used as a focus of argument. In the process of responding to it, questioning it, and modifying it, the actual formal strategy of the organization gets formed. Such is the case at AT&T's Transmission Systems Business Unit. A preliminary draft of the strategic plan is communicated to employees at all levels, and their criticisms and suggestions are solicited; by the time the final plan is approved, it incorporates many of their ideas.

More people than ever before are working together to arrive at a shared understanding of the business and its direction. This is essentially part of the learning taking place in the organization and a way to synthesize the creative energies and knowledge of people at all levels.

AVOIDING MANAGEMENT BURNOUT

Despite the fact that many companies are looking for ways to retain their most valued employees, many others are being forced to pare their workforces. "Downsizing is the Wall Street fad of the 1990s," a recent *Wall Street Journal* piece proclaimed.[12] In the course of layoffs and restructurings, many, many management positions have been permanently eliminated. Their management work has been taken up by teams of all sorts, who now regularly handle such administrative duties as scheduling, hiring and even performance appraisals.

Advanced information systems perform much of the information gathering and synthesis formerly done by managers. The newest wave of technology is groupware, software programs designed to give people throughout the organization information they need to work together. "Everyone in a company's many departments has access to the same data, in a common format, and to all updates," a press release for a new groupware product boasts. "By giving workers well below the top of the organizational pyramid access to information previously unavailable or restricted to upper levels of management, groupware spreads power more widely than before,"[13] *Fortune* reports.

The next logical step is to distribute some of the planning work of management to others in the organization as well. This is not only a "nice" thing to do in terms of empowerment; it's a practical and necessary step to avoid burning out the managers who remain. "There's just not slack any more," maintains one manager we interviewed who starts work at 7 A.M. and may not leave until 10 P.M. When we thanked him for submitting to an interview late on a Friday, he seemed genuinely surprised: "Oh, it's only 5:00 P.M. That's not the end of the day."

At General Electric, revenues have risen 150 percent in the last ten years, while the number of people employed fell by 43 percent. "Initially, at GE, middle managers were dying," Noel Tichy, a consultant who helped with the transformation, recalled. "The middle managers were saying things like, 'I know adding head-count isn't the answer, but I'm working seven days a week trying to do all the old things and it isn't working.'"[14]

Managers, who may now have up to twenty to forty people reporting directly to them, simply can't continue to do things the old way. Decision-making is being pushed farther and farther down the organization chart. In GE's medical systems group, it once took eight signatures to get a replacement part for a hospital's magnetic resonance imaging system. Now, no signoffs are required. Marriott has given increased responsibility to its Guest Services Associates, who are authorized to do whatever it takes to get travelers into the hotel and settled quickly and happily. At Pepsi, field reps now design marketing and promotions directly with their customers, without needing to get approvals. If you are tempted to dismiss these changes as mere tactics, remember: Tactics can often drive strategy, rather than the other way around. Increased power to make decisions means more opportunities to affect the actual strategies of the organization through the evolution of new approaches.

IT'S HAPPENING ANYWAY

What we call strategy-making is not a recent phenomenon. Successful strategies have always been partly the result of formal planning and partly evolutionary. They have balanced the human need for direction, order, and predictability with the recognition that life rarely works as planned.

However, with people at all levels taking on increased responsibility, strategies are emerging—instead of being formulated in advance—more frequently than ever before. And because of the increasingly fast pace of change, it is becoming more important for organizations to be on the lookout for evolving strategies and to capitalize on them.

In many organizations, people at all levels are already making strategy. Some are doing it consciously; others are not aware of the strategic implications of their actions. Remember the product development team at General Motors responsible for development of the Aurora model? In 1990 the recession and GM's poor sales forced the car maker to suspend several new-car projects, including what was then called the G-car.

The team charged with development of the vehicle stuck to the letter of the order but not the spirit. "We kept on doing research even though we didn't have the tooling money," Douglas Stott recalls. "We had a futuristic and appealing design, so the delay didn't hurt us, fortunately. We knew we'd get the car, we just didn't know when." When market and internal cash positions shifted two years later, the Aurora became the cornerstone of GM's product strategy.

In a similar case, the IBM Research Division continued with a project that had long been opposed by the company's mainframe computer executives. The mainframers were afraid that parallel-processing supercomputers, which could operate independently of a mainframe, would hurt their sales.

The Research Division had a very different idea of where parallel computing was going. Using its own moneys, it developed the product between December 1991 and February 1993. "We actually built the first couple of manufacturing prototypes here in the research lab because that was the fastest way to get there," the division's director, James McGroddy, reports.[15] When it became evident that this new generation of products was indeed what the market wanted, IBM Research was there with the product.

In the mid 1980s, managers in the Manufacturing Division of what is now The Geon Company believed strongly that the company would only gain a competitive advantage if it was able to boast a low cost position. This strategy was at odds with the formal strategy at the time, which emphasized the provision of value-added products and services. "At one point," reports Ed Wiseman, Director of Management and Organizational Development, "Manufacturing had even developed their own plan outside of the official business plan."

The Manufacturing plan called for lowering costs by consolidating the number and type of raw materials used and minimizing the number of different kinds of products each production line had to run. "We got resistance like you couldn't believe," remembers manufacturing director Glenn Higby. "By the late '80s, we started to emphasize how manufacturing could help profitability by increasing run rates and avoiding unnecessary overtime and so on. We contended that the way you really add value is to make a good product cheaper. We figured out a way to say it so that people started to get on board."

Now Geon has embraced the low-cost producer strategy fully, with outstanding results. "This strategy was developed in a highly iterative way over a long period of time," notes Higby. "I compare it to a sailboat race; you have a plan, but it changes to take advantage of the opportunities and challenges you encounter as you go along."

Of course, it's harder to identify cases in which evolving strategies wasted time and money with no ultimate payoff, took the company off track, and diverted resources from more strategically important matters. But that happens, too. By recognizing the power of evolving strategies, leaders can be more vigilant about identifying and putting a stop to those initiatives that are truly detrimental to the organization's ability to compete.

Leaders who understand that strategy-making is happening everywhere in their organization can encourage initiative-taking that is aligned with strategic goals, defuse efforts that are truly at odds with the chosen strategic direction, and find ways to incorporate newly evolving strategies into the business's plans.

BUT HOW?

We suspect that few people would argue about the desirability of be-coming more market-focused and flexible, retaining skilled associates, and avoiding management burnout. In theory, it sounds pretty good. As with most things in life, the difficulty comes in the execution. In the next chapter, we'll examine some of the dilemmas that come along with making strategy everyone's job, and we'll offer some suggestions about how those dilemmas can begin to be resolved.

3

Dilemmas in Strategy-making

Damned If You Do . . .

Dilemma: 1. an argument presenting two or more alternatives equally conclusive against an opponent, 2a. a choice or a situation involving choice between equally unsatisfactory alternatives. b: a problem seemingly incapable of a satisfactory solution.
—*Webster's Dictionary*[1]

While many of the companies profiled in this book are finding ways to involve leaders at all levels in strategy-making, others are sticking with a more traditional process. With all its potential benefits, what prevents companies from adopting the more participatory approach? Inviting wider participation in strategy-making brings its own set of dilemmas that must be acknowledged and managed. A dilemma has been defined as a "situation in which conflicting aims impose tension."[2] In fact, the tension created by such dilemmas may prevent many organizations from sharing strategy-making responsibility more widely.

By their very nature, dilemmas resist obvious solutions. Len Sayles, a management researcher, puts it this way: "In a complex, changing world, most leadership challenges pose dilemmas: damned if you do, damned if you don't. . . . The need to keep adapting, shifting, rebalancing is likely to be a lot more useful than knowing the right way to do things."[3] Here are three of the main dilemmas that come with making strategy everyone's business:

- Involving more people in strategic decision-making takes *more time*. Aren't we trying to make such decisions *more quickly* in order to be more responsive to the market?
- If everyone in the organization is involved in strategy making, *who makes the final decisions? Should we be trying to eliminate hierarchy?*
- How can the organization maintain *strategic focus* if people are constantly running after *new opportunities* presented by its customers and markets?

We often think resolving a dilemma means choosing one alternative over the other. You can choose to involve more people in a decision, or you can make it quickly. You can have hierarchy, or you can have participation.

In their innovative research on organizational dilemmas, Charles Baden Fuller and Charles Hampden-Turner point out the fallacy of such a perspective. In the most successful companies, they argue, "potential conflict between objectives or courses of action has been reconciled so that each contributes positively to the other."[4] For example, management theorists once made a clear distinction between companies that pursue a strategy of economies of scale (make widgets the same way and make lots of them at the lowest cost) and companies that emphasize differentiation (make specialized widgets for specific markets and they'll pay more for them). Recently, however, some organizations have come to realize that to have a real advantage, they may have to do both simultaneously: flexible manufacturing on a large scale. This is the "mass customization" strategy that Compaq Computer is currently pursuing as it wrestles with redesigning its production process; its goal is to build computers customized to each customer's specifications within a few days of the time the order is placed. The dilemma is not resolved by choosing one alternative over the other. It is resolved by finding a way to do both at the same time.

Let's look at three common dilemmas of strategy-making in this light and suggest ways in which these apparent contradictions might begin to be reconciled.

Dilemma 1: Involving more people in strategic decision-making takes more time. Aren't we trying to make such decisions more quickly in order to be more responsive to the market?

When leaders talk about the downsides of involving more people in strategic decisions, they frequently cite time as the demon. In many organizations, inviting wider participation means more meetings, more politics, more memos, more signoffs. Leaders may fear, and rightly so, that broader involvement can lead to corporate gridlock and an inability to make responsive decisions.

However, a simple rephrasing of the question makes a world of difference. Instead of thinking of participation versus time as opposites, try asking the question this way: "How can we get more people involved in strategy-making *in order* to make decisions more quickly in response to the marketplace?"

The key to resolving this dilemma is in defining *how* people in the organization are involved in strategy-making. The role of the strategic leader is different from that of the salesperson in the field. The customer service rep will make a different contribution to the strategy process from the one the CEO will. Whatever their roles, leaders at all levels need to understand that they are part of the process, and they need to know what contribution they are being encouraged to make. We'll discuss the various roles people throughout the organization are taking in the strategy-making process in Part Two.

How are effective companies getting more people involved in strategy-making in order to make decisions more quickly and responsively? One way, paradoxically, is to get corporate executives out of the process of developing specific strategies for the business units. Hewlett-Packard is broken into global, cross-functional teams that "own" their own businesses and can react quickly to their markets. Profit and loss statements for each business help ensure that the units are not only autonomous, but accountable for results. *Fortune* summed it up this way: "H-P executives have an enviable degree of freedom. For one thing, they are authorized to reinvest the capital their businesses generate. They can attack markets in their own ways, rather than slavishly wait for orders that reduce them to just one part of a grand corporate strategy."[5]

Like Hewlett-Packard, many companies are making the transition to customer-focused cross-functional teams in order to get better decisions made faster. For example, an international cross-functional team at National Semiconductor is credited with making major changes in its packaging materials in less than six months.

In 1993 logistics experts who had been in touch with the business center outside of Munich identified what could become a significant problem. European countries were considering legislation that would require the provider of goods to arrange for the disposal of the packaging of their products. If this legislation were enacted, consumers would no longer be able to dispose of packaging materials with their regular garbage.

Without waiting for a mandate from above, the logistics people pulled together an international team of experts in environmental affairs, purchasing, quality assurance, technical documentation, and even public relations. "We knew that something was going to happen in six months," Dan Wilkowsky, who is Director of Corporate Environmental and Safety Services, recalls. "We said, 'Our customers are going to want to know what we're going to do, so we better get out there and tell them.'"

The packaging team members began by evaluating the current packaging materials and were surprised to find out that National Semiconductor was shipping a million cardboard cartons each month. The cardboard, which was recyclable, was less of a problem than other materials, namely Styrofoam and plastic bubble wrap. Within six months' time, the team led a companywide effort to change the packaging. "Thanks to the efforts of National's international packaging team, we are now using methods that make it possible for our customers to recycle more than 6 million cardboard boxes and 48 million semiconductor packaging tubes every year. National has also eliminated the use of plastic bubble packaging in Europe," Wilkowsky announced in May 1994.

One of the most widespread uses of cross-functional teams is in the area of product development. Harold Faig, the Cincinnati Milacron manager who headed the project team to develop the Vista machine, says that the drive to develop that product quickly actually created the need for the cross-functional development team. Because the company was being badly beaten in the marketplace, Faig and his colleague Bruce Kozak knew that time was of the essence. They knew also that the current sequential development process, which typically took two years, would not allow them to meet their goal. "We had to create a team concept and move away from functional management, moving away from designing something in engineering without much input from the market or the customer or anybody else. . . . It sped up the process because you don't have redundancy of functions," Faig reports.

A similar sense of urgency led Robert Hershock to create cross-functional product development teams in 3M's Occupational Health and Environmental Safety Division. That division's products help protect workers from health and safety hazards on the job. When Hershock took over as head of the division in 1983, their two core products were ten and twenty years old; patents were running out. Looking back, he describes his rationale for experimenting with one of the earliest uses of cross-functional teams: "The number one thing was that we needed new products and we had to get them to the market, because we didn't know if we were going to be in business in the future or not."

Eleven teams were chartered, each focusing on an area with good growth potential. Each team established its own goals, budgets, and deadlines. The results were impressive. Product development time was reduced by half or better. Out of the first eleven teams established, 3M got ten new products. "We came out with products that were new to the world—revolutionary products. The quality was built in at the beginning. Every product exceeded the [OSHA] regulations by at least 50 percent, and we met the competitive market prices," Hershock says.

Of course, the day-to-day decisions made by product development and customer-focused teams are only part of the business's overall strategy. For those teams to make a real impact on deliberate strategies that are typically formulated by the organization's strategic leaders, a formal but flexible system of two-way communication is needed. Organizations need ways to ensure that teams and individuals pass on important and relevant information, and to ensure that the information makes it through the maze of wastebaskets to those who are codifying the strategic direction for the business.

People who are involved in strategy-making also need to develop new skills and perspectives that will allow them to make meaningful contributions to the process. Rich Teerlink, CEO of Harley Davidson, noted somewhat wryly that "if you empower dummies, you get bad decisions faster."[6] Mark Bregman from IBM Research argues that people need two principal competencies to be valuable to strategy-making: "the breadth to understand the broad arena (not just their particular function), and the depth to be a kind of expert witness on issues in their own area." In Part Three, we describe in more detail the skills required of strategy-makers at all levels of the organization.

Finally, people at all levels need to understand current strategies and the reasons behind them so that they can make decisions consistent with the strategic focus of the firm. Which brings us to our next dilemma . . .

Dilemma 2: If everyone in the organization is involved in strategy making, who makes the final decisions? Should we be trying to eliminate hierarchy?

Wider involvement can succeed only if the traditional hierarchy of strategy-making is deemphasized; however, organizations still need a way to ensure that strategic decisions are consistent with the direction of the overall enterprise. In their book *The Seven Cultures of Capitalism*, Charles Hampden-Turner and Alfons Trompenaars sum up this dilemma very well:

> Every enterprise needs to give its employees an equality of opportunity to make valuable contributions. . . . Yet pushing every point made by every employee on every issue could result in corporate gridlock and chronically delayed decisions. For this reason employee contributions must be subjected to a hierarchy of expert judgment that combines and coordinates their use. . . . The "integrity" of the organization depends on striking a balance between the need for an *equality* of input and a *hierarchy* for judging the merits of the input.[7]

Hierarchy, defined by Webster's as "persons or other entities arranged in a series," cannot be eliminated. In many organizations today, the villain is not hierarchy per se, but *bureaucracy* —"a system of administration marked by officialism, red tape and proliferation." William McGowan, MCI's founder, has said that the biggest risk of all is that "the lean, fast-acting management style that's made the company a winner will turn into a fat-assed bureaucracy where managers spend all their time writing procedures, forming committees, attending meetings, decorating their offices, building empires, and protecting their tushes instead of making things happen."[8] Businesses that have eliminated layers of management and flattened their organizational charts are slimming down overdeveloped hierarchies, but hierarchy in itself is unavoidable.

Hierarchy, then, serves two purposes:

• Hierarchy ensures that everyone in the organization understands *who makes the final call* on unresolved issues. Instead of being limiting, this kind of clarity about decision-making can be empowering. People need to know not only what they are responsible for but also the limits of that responsibility. The challenge is to create a clear, comprehensible hierarchy that doesn't encourage people to think and behave in a limited, bureaucratic fashion.

• Hierarchy allows a large organization to be *divided into smaller component parts*. Without a formal structure or hierarchy, discrete manageable subunits would be impossible. As organizations like Asea Brown Boveri have demonstrated, such smaller units give people a greater sense of belonging and responsibility for results. Hierarchy shows how the subunits are related to each other and to the workings of the enterprise overall. The challenge is for subunits to be clear about their roles and responsibilities while at the same time being flexible enough to cross organizational boundaries to address customer needs and new opportunities.

The goal, then, is to eradicate unnecessary hierarchy and to create a culture in which hierarchy is used constructively. To rephrase the dilemma: "How can we use organizational hierarchies to empower people?"

The degree of hierarchy required for clarity, empowerment, and coordination varies from company to company, depending on:

• The nature and variety of businesses in the portfolio
• The number and type of markets that they serve

- The need for an overarching corporate identity in the minds of customers and shareholders
- The corporation's existing capital condition and the culture of the company and the units within it

Each industry, each company is different, and no single formula works for every one. One of the strategic leader's key roles is to determine what kind of decision-making process and what degree of autonomy fit the corporation's particular circumstances. Again, balance is the key. We're not talking about the choice between autocracy and chaos. We're talking about ways to balance participation and decisiveness, empowerment and responsibility.

Dilemma 3: How can we maintain strategic focus if we are constantly running after new opportunities presented by our customers and markets?

One of a leader's worst nightmares is that everyone in the organization is working diligently, but they are all working at cross purposes and the company is going nowhere. It's the corporate equivalent of the dream in which you are desperately running, but you're just running in place. The dilemma is pervasive: How do you maintain focus on key strategies and still remain open to new opportunities? How do you empower people to make decisions and still ensure that those decisions are consistent with where you want to go strategically? Xerox Chairman and CEO Paul Allaire calls this dilemma "the necessary tension between autonomy and integration."[9]

Again, the key to resolving this dilemma lies in rephrasing the question: "How can an organization maintain strategic focus *by* remaining open to new opportunities?"
This suggests two things:

- *Strategic focus is defined through a constant, ongoing dialogue* between top management and the rest of the organization about which actions are and are *not* consistent with that focus. It is through communication about which new opportunities were selected and why that people understand in a practical way exactly what the strategic focus means.

- *Strategic focus is not static;* it constantly evolves and shifts, based on new developments in the environment. Maintaining focus on a particular strategy must be balanced with constant attention to changes that may indicate a need for a shift in strategy. New opportunities provide a view of changes in the market which may be ignored by a business intent on maintaining a strict focus on the strategies it has selected.

STRATEGY AS DIALOGUE

Let's look first at the idea that strategic focus is defined for people in the organization through dialogue. As Eccles and Nohria point out, strategy is essentially language, and the broad words typically used to define a business's strategic direction are interpreted differently by different people.[10] Take, for example, the strategy of becoming a global company. The top management team may say that the company needs to become more global in scope in order to compete in a changing industry. But globalization has a wide variety of permutations. As the various business units find and evaluate opportunities in new geographical arenas, the strategy will be refined. Do we expand in areas with the biggest market potential? Do we follow existing major customers to serve them everywhere they are? Do we create relatively independent units run and staffed by foreign nationals? Do we try to export our "home country" systems and culture? Do we expand alone or through joint ventures with companies that may have more experience in these markets? Do all business units try to go global in the same way?

While the answers to those questions may be thought out in advance by senior executives, it is more likely that the answers will emerge out of action. As various approaches are tried and refined, the strategy of globalization will be shaped to fit the strengths and culture of the specific company. For example, ConAgra recently shifted its globalization strategy, closing the independent unit it created to lead its push abroad and delegating the responsibility to expand overseas to its individual companies, which best know their own businesses.[11] It is only through ongoing dialogue that people at all levels really come to understand the specific form of globalization that the business is pursuing.

This dialogue includes talk about which opportunities were pursued and which were not, the rationale behind those choices, and the ongoing status of various new ventures in different arenas. In this way, the strategy becomes more focused through the evaluation of new opportunities (rather than allowing the multitude of possible choices to lead to strategic diffusion and chaos).

STRATEGIC FOCUS AS A MOVING TARGET

Our other point about strategic focus is that it is not static. While focus can be established for the organization through the evaluation of new opportunities, the new possibilities can also have an impact on the strategic direction itself. The issue, then, becomes not just how to maintain focus but how to know when it's time to change it. Outdated or misguided focus may be worse than none at all.

IBM and Digital Equipment learned this lesson the hard way when they were left behind because of their strict strategic focus on mainframe computers. Bill Gates at Microsoft is reportedly concerned that his company not make the same mistake: "We will not fall short for not having an expansive view of how technology can be used," he said.[12]

Thermo Electron was founded with just such an expansive view. In 1956, when George Hatsopoulos incorporated the company in the same week in which he received his Ph.D., he "set out to pursue any business in which we could make a unique contribution, and which we had the technological talents and ideas to pursue." In the 1960s the company worked with NASA's space program on products related to power generation. They were also searching for other focal points, however, and initiated a project to develop an artificial heart. Sometimes the same people were working in both arenas.

When the Clean Air Act was enacted in 1970, Thermo Electron developed a completely new technology for measuring oxides of nitrogen and captured the worldwide market for this application. That innovation launched its instrumentation business, which is still one of its mainstays. When the energy crisis hit the United States two years later, the company used its expertise in thermodynamics and energy to help industrial companies be more efficient in their use of power. "The central idea," Hatsopoulos says, "is that Thermo Electron is in many lines of business. But one of the most important lines of business of Thermo Electron is finding new lines of business."

Such an expansive view can be achieved only by actively searching out new opportunities—opportunities that may or may not be consistent with existing strategies. For example, Xerox's research center in Ontario developed a highly specialized film for the graphic arts market. Because of its potential, a new business unit was established to commercialize the product. The CEO, Paul Allaire, noted, "It's not mainline. It's not part of our document strategy. But it is a technological offshoot that could be big business. . . . In the old days, this technology might never have seen the light of day."[13]

It stands to reason that when more people are on the lookout for such possibilities, more opportunities will be unearthed or generated. What today is no more than a promising development can be the basis for a major shift in strategic focus for the future.

In the chapters that follow, you'll read examples of companies that are using a number of different ways to manage the dilemmas we've discussed. Some have developed methods for getting broader input into the development of formal strategies. Others have delegated the responsibility for important day-to-day decisions—the evolutionary side of strategy—to lower levels of the organization. Whatever the method, the goal is to create organizations that are more flexible and competitive by balancing the needs for broader participation and timely response, shared authority and decisiveness, strategic focus and the exploitation of opportunities as they arise.

4

Empowerment with Teeth

Getting People Involved in the
Formal Strategy Process

American workers want more influence than they now have in many areas of company
decision-making that affect their jobs or work lives.
    —*Worker Representation and Participation Survey, 1994*[1]

As businesses search for ways to become more responsive to the rapidly changing needs of their customers and markets, many are recognizing the need to "empower" people at all levels. Empowerment as a concept in business life grew out of the Quality movement, which reached its peak of popularity in the 1980s. Current buzzwords used to describe empowerment efforts include employee involvement programs, team-based organizations, reengineered core processes, and self-directed work groups. While the intention behind these diverse and often un-connected programs is undoubtedly good, many are in real danger of being seen as "flavor of the month" solutions; if you don't agree with the program, simply ride it out—another will be along next year.

What's the problem? Don't people at all levels welcome the chance to have more input and responsibility? The problem is that, too often, empowerment is seen as an empty concept. Teams are endowed with increased responsibility for only trivial tasks; task forces recommend solutions that are vetoed by senior management because they are inconsistent with the business's direction. People in the middle of organizations are indeed caught in the middle: "My boss wants me to empower my people, but half the time, when they make a recommendation, I have to go back and tell them we can't do it."

What's missing? As we strive for more participative organizations, we've overlooked a critical element: the overall framework that can turn empowerment into a competitive advantage. Strategy provides the context that makes it possible for people at all levels to make a meaningful contribution to the business's purpose, goals, and ways of operating.

People are not truly empowered as long as they believe that the organization's strategies are being handed down from on high. They are not willing to give their full effort and commitment to what they see as autocratic and at times arbitrary shifts in strategic direction. True empowerment is possible only when people at all levels have input into the organization's strategy, when they understand the rationale behind it, when they become actual players in the strategy-making process.

THE CASE AGAINST TRADITIONAL STRATEGIC PLANNING

As organizations seek to involve more people in strategy, the logical place to start is with their formal planning processes. Traditional strategic planning—as in the analytical, top-down process so popular in large corporations for the last twenty years—has taken a beating lately. If you read management journals, you have no doubt noticed a great deal of debate about and widespread disillusionment with the very concept of strategic planning.

Managers report experiences with planning that have caused them to doubt its effectiveness as a vehicle for corporate change; they point to vast gaps between what was designed and what was delivered, or to repeated failures to achieve established goals.

Today's news pages are replete with tales of failed forecasts and the tremendous financial impact of those miscalculations. For example, when IBM announced in early October 1994 that it had sold out its new Aptiva home computers through the end of the year, costing it tens of millions of dollars of vital fourth-quarter revenue, it attributed the shortage to "conservative forecasting."

Meanwhile, various outside observers of the process argue that planning's inherently programmatic nature is at fault. The management theorist Henry Mintzberg argues astutely that strategic planning is prone to devolving into an overly rigid focus on analysis and quantification, making it innately inflexible. The traditional approach, he argues, is incapable of predicting crucial market shifts or of encouraging timely adaptation to them once they occur. Its artificially linear systems can create long time lags between intention and execution and can foster a myopic, short-term financial orientation among top managers.[2]

Other critics, including Gary Hamel and C. K. Prahalad, have pointed out that traditional strategic planning fails to take into account the creative processes and discoveries that generate breakthroughs and prompt major shifts in strategic direction.[3] Planning has been accused of stifling creativity by eliminating true vision and synthesis from the process of change. The overemphasis on rational analysis has led to the creation of strategies that are either repetitions of a largely irrelevant past or imitations of other organizations. In our attempt to institutionalize and regulate innovation through traditional strategic planning, we have, in many cases, stifled the organization's ability to renew itself.

Finally, planning has been faulted for its use as an instrument of control, particularly over middle managers; corporate planners have usurped those managers' rights to determine the direction of the units they know so intimately. Strategic planning has been characterized as, in effect, a forced march mandated from above, in which both the ultimate destination and the route to be taken are dictated before setting out; all the participants can do is march in lockstep toward the preordained goal. In this sense, it is seen as diametrically opposed to the new ethos of empowerment. The traditional process can discourage even senior managers from taking responsibility for strategy and can lead to passivity rather than dynamic responses to the situation at hand.

THE EVOLUTION—NOT THE DEATH— OF STRATEGIC PLANNING

Those criticisms are certainly valid. The traditional approach to strategic planning, formulated in a very different era, is often inadequate to deal with the rapid and continuous changes of today's marketplace. It also fails to take into account the increased demand for autonomy among members of today's workforce.

Despite academics' assertion that planning is dead, however, most organizations are resisting the temptation to discard strategic planning in its entirety. In our interviews with hundreds of managers for this book, we have never heard anyone say, "Oh, strategic planning—we don't do that any more." Even the critics of planning agree that every organization needs a sense of focus and direction. Instead of being abandoned, then, the strategic planning process is being revitalized and reshaped within a broad spectrum of companies.

Strategic planning's top-down flow and linear procedures are breaking down, just as the hierarchies of management are. What was once a structured, once-a-year activity undertaken by a single group of senior managers and planners is becoming an iterative, continuous process that involves the entire organization.

The new twist on strategic planning comes in many forms. Gleaned from our research with organizations in a wide variety of industries, here are some ways in which companies are getting more people involved in the formal planning process:

- *Moving responsibility for planning to lower levels.* In many companies, strategic plans are being developed throughout the organization, rather than solely at the corporate level.
- *Using multilevel teams for planning.* Strategic planning teams are being composed of people from various levels, not just from top management.
- *Soliciting broad input before the plan is finalized.* Plans are presented as works in progress, and opinions are sought from people at all levels before the plan is adopted.

"DOWN" WITH PLANNING: MOVING RESPONSIBILITY FOR PLANNING TO LOWER LEVELS

Delegating the responsibility for the development of formal plans to lower levels is an unheralded but very noticeable trend in U.S. businesses. In effect, many corporate executives who are responsible for their overall enterprises are getting out of the business of setting specific strategies, and are assigning that responsibility to the individual business units.

For example, before 1992 Xerox was "a classical, functional organization. There was a corporate strategy office, and strategies were done in a centralized way," according to David Myerscough, Senior Vice President of Corporate Strategy. "It was very much top-down, and there was not a lot of involvement down in the layers of the organization."

Three years after Paul Allaire took over as CEO, he asked a group of people to take a look at the "organization's architecture," and as a result Xerox reorganized itself into nine business divisions tied to specific markets. Within each division there are between two and six subgroups, or business teams. They are responsible for strategy—defining the market, understanding and determining revenue needs, keeping track of and responding to competitors. These teams are cross-functional in composition and are led by a business team general manager.

The key driver behind the reorientation was time. In a world economy, Xerox knew that it had to make decisions as quickly as possible to keep up with competitors. To do so, top executives decided to delegate responsibility for strategy-making to the units in direct contact with their markets. "We found that if time was your metric," Myerscough notes, "you had to empower those lower in the organization to make decisions. Because you've got a 16 billion dollar company, there is no way that you can run it with five people at the top making all the decisions."

Some might argue that delegating decisions to the head of a Xerox unit can hardly be considered strategy-making at lower levels, but this example illustrates a trend that is emerging and being replicated at company after company. At Rubbermaid Corporation, nearly thirty teams take responsibility for the development and marketing of specific prod-

NAPLES UNIVERSITY LIBRARY

uct lines. Each five-person cross-functional team is composed of representatives from sales, marketing, finance, manufacturing, and R&D. Each team develops its own operating and strategic plans; each is accountable for its own profitability. CEO Wolf Schmitt maintains that "this structure gives the teams a feeling of ownership and entrepreneurship" and will help Rubbermaid double its sales by the year 2000.[4]

Asea Brown Boveri, an innovative company heralded by the business press and academics alike, is divided into five thousand profit centers; again, each is responsible for its own profitability. "My boss lets me run my own business. That's what ABB is all about," says Nicholas Stroud, who runs a power-circuit plant in Greensburg, Pennsylvania. The Westinghouse plant, which was acquired by ABB in 1989, was out of the red in a year and doubled its sales within three years by following strategies developed within the unit.[5]

As you might suspect, corporate executives' role in this process involves more than simply getting out of the way of the business units. CEOs and management teams often use financial or quantitative targets as parameters to drive the process. At CSX, the bottom-line goal is for the company's return on capital to exceed the cost of capital. At 3M, the target established in 1991 called for the company to regain its status as premiere innovator by generating 30 percent of its sales from products introduced within the past four years. At Mead, the measure is 4 percent productivity gains over the prior year.[6]

Exxon uses strict financial controls, measuring all decisions against a targeted return on capital. Beyond such conservative financial management, decision-making is shifted to subsidiaries, which are given great freedom. *The Economist* reported recently that "this bottom-up approach makes Exxon surprisingly flexible, with large changes coming about almost automatically, rather than through some preordained plan imposed by the board."[7]

Other companies, such as Union Carbide, have long used variations of a top-down/bottom-up planning process. After corporate leadership establishes broad goals and targets, each business unit develops its own strategic plan. The plans are then consolidated and presented to subsequent levels of the hierarchy for review and approval.

This process has several distinct advantages, chiefly that the managers who know their businesses best are responsible for the development of the plans. However, in large, hierarchical organizations the number of approvals and signoffs required before implementation can begin often turns what might have been a flexible, participatory process into a bureaucratic, time-consuming mess. In addition, the process is too often seen as the sole responsibility of the business units' top managers, who fail to get input from people at other levels of their own organizations. Other pitfalls of such a planning process include:

- *Aggregate data may become less and less meaningful.* In a large organization, the quantitative data needed for decision-making becomes more and more aggregated as it is sent up the line for approval. That can limit the ability of senior management to understand the messages behind the numbers and to test the assumptions they are based on.
- *The process may encourage people to play The Budget Game.* While top management may agree with the goals of the various business units' plans, resources required to enact the plans may be limited. "Yes, you have the approval for the plan," they may say, "but do it with less money." Over time, then, business units begin to pad their requests for resources, knowing that they will not get everything they ask for. Corporate leaders, in turn, approve fewer resources than requested because they suspect that the units are asking for more than they need.
- *Approvals can be based more on personality than on logic.* Because proposed strategies and requests for resources are often presented in face-to-face meetings, the style and approach of the presenter can affect the likelihood of approval. In other words, a leader with a strong speaking style or with superior influence skills may have a greater chance of obtaining senior management buy-in than someone who is weak in those areas, regardless of the merits of their proposals.

While this kind of planning process has admittedly been misused in the past, we don't consider it to be beyond redemption. Where such a process is working, it is kept flexible and vital by:

- Limiting the number of levels of management that must approve the plans
- Encouraging higher levels of management to sign off on the general assumptions behind the plans and the overall strategic goals, without succumbing to the temptation to tinker with the strategies per se
- Ensuring that all people in the business units, not merely those on the top team, are involved in the process. This can be done before the actual planning session (via interviews and questionnaires) or by presenting drafts of plans and asking for comments and questions
- Discouraging voluminous documentation (Too often, the goal of the planning process shifts subtly from the creation of a set of strategic objectives to the documentation of a plan for the benefit of senior management. Overemphasis on consistency of format among what may be very different businesses can contribute to a paperwork avalanche.)

The documentation habit can be hard to break. When 3M's Robert Hershock took over as head of a traditionally hierarchical division and launched the use of cross-functional product development teams, he said to the team leaders: "There will be no reporting up the organization." "Because what happens," he recalls, "is that these people spend more time figuring out the reports than they do inventing the products. . . . I didn't want any overheads, any written reports, none of that stuff. Well, the first meeting, they all came with overheads and were going to make formal presentations. . . . You see, it was a trust issue, because you have to realize the kind of environment they were used to. It took a while to build that trust."

BREAK DOWN THE BARRIERS:
USING MULTILEVEL TEAMS FOR PLANNING

Asking business units and teams at lower levels to develop strategies, which are then approved by those at senior levels, is only one approach. It's a method that still pays homage to hierarchy and uses the hierarchy to structure wider participation. In some companies, it's the best way to go to begin involving people at all levels of the organization in the process. Some companies, however, are trying a more innovative approach to encouraging the involvement of people at all levels. They are creating multilevel teams for the sole purpose of strategic planning. Instead of automatically assigning only senior managers to such a task, they are forming strategic planning "task forces" that include people from various levels and functions.

At Komo Machines, a U.S. maker of machinery for metalworking and cabinetry, employees were invited to apply for work on the strategic planning team. About a third of them took up the invitation. Thirteen team members were selected. The team includes the President but is mostly a cross-section of people from all levels of the organization. In 1993 the team produced its first business plan. An advertising manager, Jim Ekberg, explains the rationale behind their more participatory approach: "When you start a company, you have fire in your belly. As you get bigger, you add overhead and bureaucracy, and that tends to slow things down. What we've done is break ourselves down into what we began as. There's less of a feudal system and more of the traditional American democracy."[8]

Such an innovative approach to planning seems even more surprising at what has been considered a bastion of bureaucracy, a public utility. At Northern States Power Company (NSP) in Minneapolis, the need to meet the challenges of an industry facing possible deregulation led to the establishment of a ten-member Organizational Planning Team representing all areas of the company. James Howard, Chairman, President, and CEO, describes the thinking that led him to charter the team: "We said, 'Okay, how best can we get ourselves positioned for that future, whether it comes in one year or five years?' Then we put together the best team we could, and we let them really go at it, gave them all the resources, time, and freedom they needed. Then we accepted what they did, which added a great deal of credibility to where I was coming from."

The team's goal was to recommend ways to restructure the company to succeed in its new environment. It included a union representative and several mid-level and upper-level managers, but only three members from the corporate officer level. A team with such a broad makeup will inevitably have to manage differences of opinion. The members of the NSP planning team debated, sometimes heatedly, what operations to put where, and whether or not support functions like Finance should be decentralized. They were, however, able to overcome their differences and reach consensus.

They made recommendations to the board of NSP without interference from top management; 95 percent of the suggestions were adopted intact. "Basically, everything they came up with was accepted," Howard recalls. Based on the team's recommendations, NSP's power generation business was set up as a separate unit. Geographical regions were established as profit and loss units. Information technology and communication systems were upgraded, and marketing and sales were increased substantially. "Our biggest fear," one team member, Ross Hammond, former Director of Environmental and Regulatory Affairs, recounts, "was that after we put a lot of time and effort into the reorganization plan . . . the recommendations would not get implemented. But we were really overjoyed at the plan's acceptance, and we got the fastest implementation schedule that could possibly have been done."[9]

LISTEN HARD: SOLICITING BROAD INPUT BEFORE THE PLAN IS FINALIZED

However the initial strategic plan is created, whether by a business unit with the approval of a top management team or by a multifunctional task force, the reality is that only a relatively small group of people can be involved in hammering out the actual plan. Our natural tendency toward skepticism will no doubt be fueled by the knowledge that a select group of people—no matter how they were selected—is determining our future. Therefore, it is not sufficient to involve a cross-section of people in the planning process. The process must also allow for the direct involvement of everyone in the organization.

The authors James Kouzes and Barry Posner describe each individual's need for control and input this way:

> The natural drive for autonomy in most people is what the leader is trying to tap. If you and I are sitting at a table predicting the probability of

pulling my number out of a hat, I will predict that I have a much better chance of winning if I know that it's my hand that will do the picking rather than yours (even though the odds are the same).[10]

Logistically, the only way to tap that "natural drive for autonomy" is to build plenty of opportunity for reaction and great flexibility into the process for developing and implementing strategic plans. James Howard describes how such participation was invited at Northern States Power:

> The original Organizational Planning Team was pretty well representative of the organization in many ways, but, of course, that was just the tip of the iceberg. After the overall recommendation was made, then the question became, "How do you do it, how do you implement it, and what else do you need to make all this work?" At that stage, we spawned additional teams throughout the company to deal with these questions. . . . So, the idea is that you get more people involved and you get more people talking about the strategy and questioning it, and having a chance to give their ideas, then they begin to understand that the world is changing, and we had better change as well.

Here are some other examples of how companies are getting input from a greater number of employees:

- At Levi Strauss, six thousand people were asked for their ideas about what the company should be doing differently to succeed in its markets. With that advice in hand, two hundred key managers gathered at headquarters to develop a strategic plan.
- At AT&T's Universal Card Services, all employees have the opportunity to meet with a senior executive in groups of no more than ten people to propose their ideas.
- At Ford, 170 executives were assembled in Detroit as the "Ford 2000 Project," with the goal of developing the strategies and organizational structure that will guide the automaker into the next millennium.

Many organizations are also using large-scale conferences, followed by specific feedback mechanisms, to gather input to be used for the development and refinement of strategic plans. Even—or, more accurately, especially—in the case of the need for downsizing, companies are discovering the benefits of wider involvement. Such benefits include the development of higher-quality plans that better reflect the market and the business's capabilities, greater buy-in from those responsible for implementing the plans, and a deeper understanding of the strategies throughout all levels of the organization.

At a U.S. division of a large international corporation, a broad-scale change effort based on a new vision and standards of excellence (specific measures used to track progress toward the vision) was undertaken in 1990. The effort, which involved some layoffs, was introduced at a leadership conference attended by more than ninety managers. Small groups at the conference critiqued the draft of the vision and standards, and their input was incorporated into a second draft.

But it didn't stop there. Each manager returned to his or her unit and solicited suggestions and reactions—which were recorded and sent back to senior management. Here are some examples of the feedback:

- "I believe in and have conveyed to my people the truly revolutionary opportunity this conference represented—that it was an opportunity for us to participate in a constructive, very real way in the development and implementation of a business plan."
- "Why did it take so long for management to catch up with the rumor mill? The changes have been too slow."
- "Having the organization structured to encourage informal and easy communication across lines of business and quicker, less cumbersome decision-making was especially welcomed."
- "The degree of uncertainty throughout the organization is affecting morale and decision-making."
- "The emphasis is on 'trimming'; however, no special consideration appears to be given to dedicated and term employees."
- "Why are we dismantling a delivery system that isn't broken? Our heretofore excellent results may be impaired by limited locations and the new 15 percent Return on Capital requirement."
- "It was difficult to characterize any broad sentiment. Some people

are experiencing a considerable amount of tension, a feeling of anger and disappointment with the organization. Others see this as an opportunity; their only concern is that they will not be recognized for their skills and their ability to learn."

These comments illustrate both the difficulties and the benefits of soliciting input from the organization. On the one hand, input that criticizes their initiatives is often very difficult for senior managers to hear. After all, a great deal of time, energy, and thought had gone into the creation of the plans presented. On the other hand, that input—both that related to the content of the proposed plan and that involving the emotions generated by the change—was critical to the success of the strategies being discussed. The feedback was used to revise plans in order to address concerns and to find ways to manage the consequences of such a major change on morale and employee retention.

Conferences such as this one are useful only if they provide a forum for *two-way* communication. We hear from people in many organizations that they have attended too many sessions consisting of a speech by the CEO followed by the presentation of plans by various senior managers. No matter how logical the plans, no matter how fancy the slides, people will not commit fully to the implementation of a strategy based on even a rousing speech.

In leading-edge companies, plans are often presented as works in progress, not completed documents. While some presentation of preliminary plans is unavoidable, senior management should use assemblies as opportunities to listen hard, rather than as forums for speechmaking. Greg Swindell of AT&T Universal Card Services says, "It is really pretty basic. You either value associate or employee input or you don't. And if you value it, you will take the time to listen." In his book *Motivation in the Real World,* Saul Gellerman describes what "listening hard" means:

> It means knowing which experiences have shaped the assumptions of the people you are listening to. It means recognizing the logic of their views, once those assumptions have been granted. Listening hard means doing your level best to get inside someone's head in order to view the world through their

eyes. Until you can present a defensible case for those views, no matter how much they differ from your own, you haven't listened hard enough.[11]

CONFERENCES: GETTING INPUT

Gathering input from people in a large conference setting can be challenging. There is little to be gained from extended, unstructured question-and-answer periods for groups of more than thirty people. However, with a bit of forethought and preparation, there are effective and efficient ways to get people's input in such a forum. Here are some suggestions:

• After the proposed strategies have been presented, break the large group into smaller table groups. Give them a format for discussing their reactions to the plans: what they liked, what their concerns are. Ask them to take some time (thirty to forty-five minutes, for example) to discuss their reactions and to prepare a brief report-out on a flipchart listing their top three "plusses" and concerns. Return to the large group, and have one representative from each table give a brief summary of their conclusions. After the conference, gather up the flipchart pages and use them to refine the strategies.

• Hold a structured question-and-answer session. Before the session, ask people to submit their questions in writing. This gives those who will answer the questions time to prepare and can eliminate redundant discussions. It also helps avoid "sandbaggers," people who ask hostile, nonconstructive questions with the sole purpose of seeing top management sweat. The disadvantage of this format is that it can underscore a feeling of mistrust and bolster the fear that management is hiding something.

• Provide structured, brief questionnaires designed to gather reactions and suggestions about the strategies. These can be completed anonymously, if your culture has traditionally discouraged honest, critical feedback, but this approach works better when the respondent is identified. This way, people can be contacted to get a better understanding of the issues and to provide information about how they are being addressed.

• Give conference participants a format and materials for holding a meeting with people in their organization who have not attended the session. This can include handouts and/or transparencies to help them explain the proposed strategies to others, questions to generate open and constructive discussions, and a suggested format for relaying suggestions and questions back to the strategy formulation team by a specific date.

• Ask conference participants to volunteer for postconference task forces to solve specific problems or tackle sticky issues.

Gathering a wide variety of input is critical. However, it can never be seen as an end in itself—a way to manipulate people's commitment by pretending they are involved. The input must actually be used. Asking for input without using or at least responding to it can be worse than not asking at all. As he described the fears of team members who were asked to make recommendations to a senior management team, William Moffett, a former team member at FMC Corporation, was eloquent:

> If, as sometimes happens in business, management had simply listened, thanked us for our work and buried our reports, then teamwork . . . would have been exposed as an illusion: teamwork is fine for planning the Christmas Dinner/Dance but not for significant decision-making.[12]

Follow-up communications after the conference should include specific, detailed responses to the ideas generated—which are being implemented, which are not, and why. Specific members of the planning committee can take on responsibility for following up on particular issues. At the end of the conference, inform people who will be following up, and by what date they can expect an update on a particular project or issue. Finally, make sure that those commitments are met.

BUILDING A PARTICIPATORY CULTURE

Regardless of the methods used to get wider participation, these efforts depend on a company culture that welcomes challenges to the status quo and encourages constructive debate. Corporate leaders need to set an example by personally demonstrating openness to new ideas and criticism. They also need to reward people at all levels for those qualities.

In many companies, this change in culture is difficult. People who have seen the shootings of numerous bearers of bad news may not be eager to volunteer for the role. It takes a concerted effort over a period of time for people to believe that their input, both positive and negative, is desired and is going to be taken seriously.

One senior executive described the challenge this way:

> Often, what we expect is for individuals to make a paradigm shift when everything else in their environment is consistent with the old ways of doing business. It's like taking someone who is righthanded and saying, "From here on out, I want you to use your left hand to get work done." But you put them in a work environment where things are geared to righthanded people.[13]

All the organization's systems must also, in time, be shifted to emphasize the goal of broader participation. Systems for performance appraisals, rewards, training, and communication all need to encourage strategy-making by every member of the business. In your organization, are people below the management level trained, evaluated, or rewarded for their ability to think strategically or for their willingness to challenge conventional wisdom? Are leaders provided with feedback on their openness to new perspectives? Does the company culture welcome people who question what the organization does and why, or are they seen as troublemakers?

Many changes are required if strategy is truly to become everyone's business. Wider involvement in the formal process is only one approach. Organizations are also finding ways to capitalize on the strategies that are continually evolving at all levels—actions taken outside the formal planning process that may have future strategic implications. Although it may seem paradoxical, companies are planning ahead to allow strategies to emerge. In the next chapter, you'll find examples of companies that are encouraging the evolution of strategies at all levels and finding ways to capitalize on them.

5

Structured Improvisation

Planning for Strategies to Emerge

Being good in business is the most fascinating kind of art.
                            —*Andy Warhol*[1]

If you've ever watched a skilled group of actors improvising a scene, you have seen a good example of how strategies evolve. Just as businesses may start with a formal plan, improvisational groups generally start with a preselected scenario—let's say, a group of four people in a waiting room. They then ask audience members for suggestions: What are these people waiting for? What do they do for a living? What are their individual characteristics?

Depending on the audience's responses, the characters could become three pregnant women and one kangaroo waiting for a doctor, or extraterrestrials applying for the U.S. space program, or hyperactive kids outside the principal's office. The actors, masters in the art of emergence, may start with a few prescripted lines. However, they soon launch into a scene in which each response is crafted on-line, based on what has happened immediately before. As in life, the endpoint is often unknown—the art is found in responding creatively to events as they transpire.

In a similar way, effective companies are becoming more improvisational in their approach to strategy. There are some interesting parallels between improvisation in the theater and the new forms of strategy-making evolving in organizations. In the past, corporate strategy-makers have, in effect, developed a detailed "script" for the organization to follow. Planners have determined in advance the optimal approach to markets, the keys for keeping customers happy, the ways to beat competitors. While such a scripted method may work in a more traditional play on stage (and in a more predictable environment in business), most theater is a one-way event—the actors present the story, the audience watches. In the business world, however, customers respond, competitors innovate, and the situation changes before the "script" or plan can play out. Strategy-makers, therefore, are becoming much less like playwrights and much more like improvisers.

Now, improvisation carries with it some connotations that may be misleading. Webster's defines "to improvise" as "to compose, or spontaneously compose and perform, on the spur of the moment and without any preparation." In reality, while the actors' technique may not be obvious, they are not without some structure or plan. They start with a scenario that they know will offer interesting possibilities. If they are an experienced ensemble, they have some idea from their past work together how the other actors will respond. Each may have a favorite line or joke that he or she works in, regardless of the specific scenario. The group often has a fall-back plan to rescue them if the scene begins to fall flat. Skilled improvisers usually have years of training and experience that allow them to respond in a seemingly effortless and creative way. They begin with a plan and with a set of shared assumptions, but their preparation, training, and experience give them the confidence to let the plan evolve.

Organizations are also finding ways to plan for strategies to evolve. They are discovering how to ensure that new situations and needs are recognized and how their systems, processes, and cultures must change to allow them to respond flexibly to new opportunities. They are learning to improvise, but it's improvisation with a structure.

The structure is provided by the organization's purpose and overall strategic direction, a set of shared assumptions about goals and values. The common purpose and the shared view of the business bind people together and form the framework that allows meaningful strategies to emerge. The success of improvisational strategy-making also relies on the skills of the organization's leaders at all levels—skills built through years of experience and training.

Leaders are encouraging the evolution of strategy in two important ways. First, they are delegating decision-making authority to people at lower levels of the organization. As people feel more free to act in response to customer needs, they make more and more decisions that may have strategic impact. In essence, they become on-line strategists—experts on a specific customer, market, or process. Second, companies are asking for more and more direct input from customers, gathered via surveys, customer forums, and joint planning sessions. Those real-time data provide an objective and thorough picture of shifting customer needs and expectations—needs that can be addressed responsively only by allowing strategies to evolve.

DELEGATING DECISION-MAKING AUTHORITY TO LOWER LEVELS

There is a growing awareness among managers and theorists that the people with the most contact with customers are a vital—and often untapped—source of differentiation between competitors in the same market. These are the people who discover the information and make the daily decisions that prompt the emergence of new strategies. Especially in service businesses, but increasingly in other sectors, companies are recognizing that people on the front lines have the most visceral effect on customers' perceptions of the business—and the most direct line to changes in the market that prompt the evolution of new strategies.

For example, salespeople can be one of your best sources of information about customers' needs and competitors' capabilities. On a daily basis, they are tuned in to who is buying what and why. Customer and technical service reps know what problems customers are having with your products and services; they hear the complaints about their quality and difficulty of use. Product development teams, which are often composed of people from various disciplines and functions, are, in effect, mini-strategy teams, targeting innovation to specific markets.

In addition to being invited to participate in formal strategic planning, people at all levels are being included in the collective strategy-making process in a less direct but equally important way. They are being encouraged to take action that can evolve into strategy. They are taking initiative to solve customers' current and potential problems online, bypassing bureaucratic signoffs and delays. This increased power to act is absolutely essential for the emergence of new strategies grounded in market needs. Think back to our analogy of the improvisational actor: The scene works only if the actor has the power and skills to respond immediately. Imagine the difference if he or she were required to get the director's approval before saying the next line.

Companies that are successfully delegating decision-making power to lower levels are doing more than paying lip service to the concept—they are working diligently and creatively to ensure that they hire the right people, that they train them well, and that the input they gather from customers is used appropriately and consistently.

Customer service representatives have been the most widely recognized segment of this front-line population. Over the past ten years, companies have been training customer contact people in the skills they need to provide excellent service. However, customer service is only part of the equation. People in a wide variety of functions—from sales to R&D to billing to marketing—are also part of the vital pipeline linking your business to your customers. Southwest Airlines' Herb Kelleher (a CEO who has been revered by the popular press as a lone hero) puts it this way:

> The people who are out there in the field, on the front lines . . . they're the ones who make things happen, not us. The people out there are the experts. You can compare our roles in the front offices to the military: we're the supply corps, not the heroes. We supply the heroes, period. The heroes are out there.[2]

To tap the skills and knowledge of those heroes, many organizations are reorganizing front-line people into customer-focused teams. At AT&T

Global Information Solutions (formerly NCR), a research project aimed at identifying customers' needs and expectations created four teams. Each worked closely with a key customer to solve problems and respond to emerging needs. Three of the customers were based in the United States; one was in Latin America.

The teams were made up of eight to ten people each, drawn from the functions that needed to work together in the service of that specific customer. They initially convened for a five-day meeting. The first two days were devoted to providing team members with the skills and perspectives they needed to work well in a team setting. On the third day, a representative of the key customer spent four to six hours responding to questions about what they wanted from the company, identifying relationship opportunities and open issues, and discussing how past decisions had affected their relationship with and perception of Global Information Solutions.

Using that information, the team created a customer relationship plan, outlining specific action steps to resolve issues and enhance the relationship with that customer. Each team member took responsibility for specific action steps, and they agreed to meet again with the customer on a quarterly basis to review progress.

Craig Lotz, who describes himself as a "process owner," talked about the initial results of the experiment: "We found that the efforts of these teams were very significant, the output was very significant. Customer satisfaction went up dramatically; team members felt as though they were really participating in solving customer problems. They felt as though they were really contributing to our desired goal state."

Interestingly, that initial research and problem-solving project evolved into a strategic restructuring of the entire organization. Based on the success of those teams, the executive committee decided to reorganize the company around what they call the "customer focused business model." They expanded the process to include virtually all customer teams, which number approximately 540.

The teams have increased authority to take action related to their customers. "In our old structure," Lotz recalls, "if a team or a sales district wanted to make a decision on behalf of the customer, they typically had to go up the flagpole and back down again. In this new model, we have put as much decision-making power as possible at the team level. The team has a better understanding of the challenge and of the impact of the decisions."

Southwest's Herb Kelleher elaborates on the notion that those with the hands-on experience are in the best position to evaluate the feasibility and ramifications of decisions:

> Before you implement an idea that has been generated in the office, you should always take it to the field and ask for their criticisms. Pretty soon the idea will look like swiss cheese—full of holes. They know what they're doing and we don't. They'll know right away, "This won't work, that won't work, let me tell you why, this won't fit that." And they get it all right! "You can do it, but not the way you're talking about."[3]

Southland Corporation has instituted a program called Accelerating Inventory Management (AIM), which was designed to put more decision-making power into the hands of its 7-Eleven store managers. "Before this, we had no say about what we needed in our store," manager Bob Price says. "The company just said, 'This is a good item, we've authorized it for our stores—boom—send five to every store.' It was just automatically shipped." Price's clerks now track inventory and daily sales on a hand-held computer and use the data, along with their intimate knowledge of their community and customers, to place orders. "Before," Price recounts, "we were just the ants out there moving the mound where we were told. Now we are seeing that the mound would never move without us, and we are actually making the decisions on moving."

Obviously, effective delegation of decision-making authority involves more than simply saying to people, "You decide." Delegating is one of the most difficult leadership practices for many managers; it means giving up some degree of control and trusting that others will do the job as well as you can (a challenge for many of us). Despite the difficulty, delegating has always been a critical part of managerial work, and it is becoming more critical all the time.

DELEGATING EFFECTIVELY

Building a culture that is comfortable with delegation begins with the organization's leaders. If leaders delegate frequently and effectively, they serve as a role model for others to do the same. If, on the other hand, they are reluctant to give people real authority to make important decisions, they limit not only people's job satisfaction but the unit's ability to be responsive to the market.

Leaders, therefore, should ask themselves—and, more importantly, ask people in their units—how frequently they:

- Give people authority to make important decisions and implement them without prior approval
- Present a strategy or policy in general terms, and then ask people to determine specific steps for implementing it
- Encourage people to determine for themselves the best way to accomplish an objective

How do leaders know if they are delegating enough? A leader may want to consider delegating more if she finds that people in her unit refer to her frequently for routine decisions, realizes that decisions are not being made when she's not around, or feels that she does not have enough time to get her own work done on a regular basis. Such was the case at Becton Dickinson, a maker of high-tech medical equipment. Following a 1990 restructuring, middle managers were swamped by an ever increasing workload. "After about a year of this," Vice President Jim Wessel says, "they said, 'I can't go on.' And then they started delegating."[4]

People who avoid delegating decisions and work often know that they should do so and would welcome the relief from the overwork that goes hand in hand with the fear of delegation. It's not that they don't want to delegate, but often they just don't know *how* to do it well. If that is true in your organization, training can help managers understand that delegation doesn't mean abdication. Based on twenty years of research by Dr. Gary Yukl, a leader in the field of effective management practices, here are some guidelines for delegating responsibility to people who report to you:

- *State responsibilities clearly and make sure they are understood.* Explain clearly what the goals of the effort are, what results you expect, and, if it's a specific project, what the deadline for completion is. Ask questions to make sure that the person understands what you have said. If the person is inexperienced or the project is very complex, you may want to review action plans before they are implemented. Clarity must, however, be balanced with the freedom to improvise. Be clear about what the objective is, but avoid telling people *how* to accomplish it.

• *Specify the limits of discretion.* A senior executive put it this way: "The leadership role is to stimulate and channel, which I interpret to mean providing the parameters and some of the limits as well as the encouragement."[5] When delegating new responsibilities, specify clearly the person's or team's limits of discretion—what you expect them to decide for themselves and the kinds of decisions you need to approve. Such authority includes the right to make decisions without prior approval and the right to use funds, equipment, materials, facilities, and other people's time.

• *Get them involved.* Dean Rusk once said, "One of the best ways to persuade others is with your ears—by listening to them." People will feel more committed if they have a say in how much authority they will have. Get them involved in deciding the limits of their discretion, and don't force them to take on more responsibility than they are comfortable with. If someone is reluctant to assume more decision-making authority, delegate responsibility gradually, allowing the person to build confidence in his or her abilities.

Peter H. Coors, President of Coors Brewing Company, describes the initial reluctance that may greet you as you ask people to take on increased responsibility: "The initial reaction of employees was to be flabbergasted and a bit uncomfortable with the freedom to do things the way they wanted. But once they became involved, the excitement, enthusiasm, and—after we accomplished the task—the pride . . . was well worth the effort and time it took to involve them."[6]

After the delegation discussion, take time to:

• *Inform others who need to know.* Tell the people who are affected by the shift in authority, including other people who report to you, peers in other units, your boss, and clients and suppliers. Unless you inform them, these people may have doubts about who is making the decisions.

• *Monitor progress.* You may assume, wrongly, that once decisions are delegated, you will be "out of the loop." This couldn't be farther from the truth. It's important to check on progress and to provide people with feedback. Together, you should decide how you will track performance and progress toward goals.

• *Provide the information they need.* In order to make decisions, people may need additional information. If possible, arrange for such information to flow directly to the people involved, instead of going through you first. Help people establish their own sources of essential data through networking, news services, etc.

• *Give support and help, but avoid "reverse delegation."* Be supportive, especially when people are discouraged or frustrated. However, when they come to you with problems related to the delegated project, avoid the very human temptation to jump in with your solution. Instead, ask them to give their recommendations and ideas for how the problem could be solved. Avoid "reverse delegation," where you reassert control over decisions that have been delegated. You can help people evaluate whether or not their solutions are feasible, but your role should remain that of a resource and consultant, not a decision-maker.

• *Make mistakes a learning experience.* When people take on new responsibilities, mistakes are inevitable. Be prepared to deal with them constructively. Accountability is one thing, perfection is another. Treat mistakes and failures seriously, but avoid responding with criticism and blame. Focus on the reasons for the mistake and ways to avoid similar problems in the future.

By improving your own delegation skills and encouraging others in your organization to do the same, you spread responsibility for taking meaningful action to a greater number of people. That allows more strategies to evolve. As people have more freedom to work with customers to solve problems and address needs, they generate more creative solutions. Those solutions, in turn, may form the kernel of future strategies.

INFORMATION FUNNELS

Of course, delegation on its own is not enough. Organizations need formal ways to ensure that information gathered by front-line strategists is funneled into the formal strategy process. After all, strategies have been evolving within organizations for as long as there have been organizations. Companies have not always been able, however, to recognize emerging strategies and to capitalize on them. What you need is a way to gather and take advantage of the information coming into the organization via people at all levels. Information sharing can take many forms:

• *Convene forums that give front-line people face-to-face access to formal strategy-makers on a regular basis.* At Philips Electronics, employees present new ideas directly to a top executive committee for approval. Lower-level managers previously had often blocked new ideas from reaching key decision-makers. "We're bringing top decision-makers to bear on new ideas so something terrific doesn't die on the vine," executive vice president Frank Carrubba says.[7]

At Mt. Bachelor Ski and Summer Resort, round tables are held every two weeks. President David Marsh; Ann Smith, VP of Human Resources; and other senior executives meet with six to ten employees from various departments and levels in an open forum. At a recent round table, the group was discussing how to make the season opening run more smoothly. Smith says: "One young woman made a suggestion about our ticketing system. We're all sitting there thinking, 'Oh, yeah—that's so obvious.' But we never thought of it because we're not out there on the front lines actually handling it."

• *Set up suggestion systems specifically for the communication of information gathered from customers.* At AT&T's Universal Card Services, which won the Baldrige award only two years after its inception, employee suggestions feed into the planning process. In the first nine months of 1992, people throughout the organization submitted more than 6,200 suggestions (up from 1,700 in 1990). Nearly half of the suggestions were accepted and acted upon.

For example, after several years of phenomenal success with adding new accounts (Universal Card holders went from 0 in 1990 to 15 million in 1994), UCS employees suggested that the business needed a more aggressive program to keep current customers. "While we still had the best retention rates in the industry," Greg Swindell, Chief Quality Officer, recalls, "our associates thought that we could be doing a better job—they gave us lots of feedback. Based on this feedback, a team was assembled whose main objective is to focus on customer retention. When appropriate, they take over calls from the customer service representatives, take time to explain the benefits of the various products and services, and do a lot of listening to current customers."

At the Ritz-Carlton Hotel Company, another Baldrige award winner in the same year, each hotel produces a daily quality production report. In this report, front-line employees identify the things they or their customers consider barriers to top-quality service. The report is distributed each day to all members of the hotel staff. Once a year, the hotels identify those issues requiring a revised overall approach for the entire company, and top management selects the most critical projects. "We have a process by which we screen the projects," Patrick Mene, VP and Director of Quality, reports. "Is it important to the customer? How big is the problem? Can we control it?" Following this screening process, Ritz-Carlton management charters cross-functional teams to deal with the problems that have been identified.

• *Provide frequent and informal access to management by encouraging gatherings of people from all levels.* Access can be limited by company practices that segregate senior managers from employees by isolating their workspaces (the executive floor) and gathering places (the executive lunchroom).

• *Use formal systems that ask people to detail their projects and activities on a regular basis.* At IBM Research, researchers submit project descriptions annually; these descriptions outline current work they are doing outside the scope of the division's formal projects.

• *Establish an ongoing task force,* such as the Customer Listening Post

Team at AT&T's Universal Card Services, which evaluates the effectiveness of its procedures for gathering, responding to, and evaluating customer comments and survey results.

This sort of feedback mechanism helps the people involved in the organization's formal planning process to recognize evolving market trends and emerging strategies. Such systems are most effective when accompanied by corresponding methods for keeping people updated on how their input is being used and by recognition and reward systems that reinforce people for providing such information.

Front-line people in your organization are a critical link in the communication chain between your company and your customers and markets. They are not, however, the only source of such information. Companies are exploring even more direct ways of soliciting customer input, which in turn suggests the need for new and evolving strategies.

GETTING CUSTOMER INPUT

Organizations are using a variety of ways to ensure that feedback from customers and other external stakeholders is incorporated into their strategic plans. At AT&T's Transmission Systems Business Unit, a draft strategic plan is circulated not only to employees but also to key suppliers for their suggestions. In addition, TSBU has established a series of customer focus groups and forums during which the unit shares its plans about its future technical direction with customers, and customers explain their own long-term plans and expectations.

As a consumer and a business professional, you have no doubt noticed the increased use of customer surveys as a way of gathering input. Surveys arrive in your mailbox weekly, often with enticements to respond, such as a dollar bill or a chance to win a prize. In your last hotel room, you may have noticed a survey on a card next to the TV listings. Suppliers may send a questionnaire to you each year, asking you to comment on the quality and reliability of their services.

The proliferation of surveys stems from businesses' growing curiosity about how they are perceived in the marketplace and their desire for hard data about their own strengths and weaknesses. In addition to the internal funnel of information about customer needs (but not *instead* of it), surveys can provide valuable information and input on the strategies that need to evolve.

The Chevrolet Division of General Motors uses a variety of surveys to measure its progress toward the goal of "Total Customer Enthusiasm." Data gathered through surveys of customers, dealers, and employees drive the identification of requirements and expectations. This allows the organization to focus on key strategic issues, which are then addressed by cross-functional teams. People at all levels of the Chevrolet organization volunteer to serve on the teams. Jack Powers, Manager of Internal Customer Processes, estimates that 300–400 employees are serving on one of these teams at any one time. Customer, dealer, and employee surveys help the organization recognize and respond to shifts in expectations. "What delights customers today," Powers observes, "may be their minimum expectations five years from now."

Another organization that conducts comprehensive, ongoing customer surveys is the Canadian Imperial Bank of Commerce's Investment and Corporate Banking business. Its initial customer survey was conducted in the fall of 1991. Allyn Keiser, who was then Executive Vice President of the Corporate Bank, describes why they decided to use such a survey: "While commissioned industry survey reports already provided us with a good idea of CIBC compared with other banks in the eyes of the market, we needed more direct information on what CIBC's customers wanted from a bank, and how well the bank was meeting those needs."

People in all areas of the bank were asked for their input into the construction of the survey. Once the questionnaire was finalized, data were gathered through more than forty face-to-face interviews and nearly 450 questionnaires mailed to customers in twenty-six industry segments. Questions covered customers' satisfaction with relationship management; pricing and structure; product breadth and value; customer service and operations; and image and reputation, and focused on how CIBC compared with its competitors.

Based on the information provided by customers, six pivotal aspects of the business relationship were identified—the "key drivers of customer satisfaction." These were the areas CIBC's customers said the bank should focus on:

- Understanding customers' goals, strategies, and businesses
- Reducing the turnover of relationship managers
- Increasing responsiveness and decreasing turnaround time
- Offering innovative proposals and creative suggestions on how to solve problems
- Balancing customers' needs with those of CIBC
- Using product managers more effectively

Many companies take surveys; fewer use the results actually to drive their strategy. CIBC took the survey results and made significant changes in the way it did business. In effect, new strategies began to evolve based on the bank's response to the customer needs identified in the survey.

For example, in order to use product managers more effectively, management devised a way to monitor how often those specialists were brought in on customer calls. Relationship managers, the key customer contact people, were encouraged to invite product managers on calls when appropriate. Top management asked product and relationship managers to use the surveys as the basis for developing joint action plans, which were then reviewed with customers for their reactions and suggestions. Training programs helped relationship and product managers manage the issues inherent in such collaboration. The bank's relationship development process, which provides a structured way to discover what customers need and how the bank can help, was also significantly enhanced.

In addition, CIBC took steps to link performance evaluations and compensation to customer satisfaction. The existing performance appraisal process was modified to include customer satisfaction measures and targets. Those targets were developed in a collaborative way between each manager and his or her direct reports. The targets are concrete, measurable ways in which each CIBC employee can be and should be satisfying customer needs.

The survey results were also the impetus for the development of ongoing systems to track progress toward meeting customer needs. A new "Customer Satisfaction Indicators" report displayed data related to the key drivers of satisfaction, including the type and number of sales calls, the number of proposals submitted to clients, the number of internal referrals, and the use of product managers. Al Keiser commented on the importance of that information:

> In many ways, these indicators are more important than financial results. In the business of relationship banking, where customers are developed over a long period of time, financial results are important to the extent that they show us how we did several years ago. The Customer Satisfaction Indicators, on the other hand, give us real-time information on how we're doing.

CIBC provides a prime example of how customer input can be used to prompt the evolution of strategy. A process in which so many diverse parties are involved, none of whom have direct authority over each other, necessarily becomes more fluid. This is strategy-making rather than planning per se—strategy evolves through constant give-and-take and iteration instead of being formulated via analysis alone.

THE ABC'S OF CUSTOMER SURVEYS

Surveys of customers can take many different forms. They can be conducted via paper-and-pencil questionnaires, telephone or face-to-face interviews, or customer focus groups. Whether you already have a survey process in place or are considering such an effort, here are some guidelines that will increase the likelihood of gathering complete and accurate information from your customers:

- The process should be simple, flexible, and cost-effective. If your buyers are a very diverse population, consider using various methods to reach different target groups.

- Surveys should ask customers to rate performance in specific categories but should also include their perceptions of importance: "Which of these areas is most important to you?" This can help you target areas for improvement that will have the most impact on customer satisfaction. For example, if customers rate your business low on product innovation but don't consider it particularly important, it may not be a high priority for improvement.
- The entire survey process should allow for broad input and ownership. Get people at all levels involved in selecting how the information should be gathered, what questions you will ask, who will be surveyed, and how the results will be presented and used.
- The process should be driven by the desire to produce results—changes in the way your business does business—rather than the need to produce reports and documentation.
- Don't ignore the power of personal interviews with key customers. They not only provide qualitative information to support the more quantitative data from written questionnaires but also give important clients a sense that you value their business and care about serving them well.
- Whatever format you choose, you should leave room for open-ended responses (for example, ask, "What suggestions do you have for how we could serve you better?") in addition to multiple-choice formats. While this makes the data analysis more difficult, the open-ended responses often provide the most valuable information.
- If you use written questionnaires, make the questionnaires anonymous, but give respondents the choice of identifying themselves if they have a specific problem to be solved and want a response.
- Consider using an outside firm to conduct the survey, to reassure customers that their individual responses will be kept confidential and will not jeopardize their relationship with you.

However you gather the information, the most important factor is what you do with it. Make sure that it can be sorted or crunched in a variety of ways. You may want to have breakdowns of data for specific units, functions, products, or locations. Then be sure to feed the data back to everyone in the organization. Let people in the Cincinnati office know what their customers think of the service they provide. Give Distribution feedback on how it, as a unit, is satisfying customers.

And set targets for improvement. What are the most important areas for focus over the next year? What rating should customers be giving us in this area a year from now? How are we going to reach that target? In the process of answering such questions and implementing the improvements, strategies emerge. Most important, these strategies are prompted by an accurate reading of customers' needs, not by internal guesswork.

Once the targets have been set, it is important to allow the actual strategies for reaching them to evolve. The targets provide the goal, the structure. Reaching the goal will require improvisation, as people in the organization discover what works and what doesn't. Encouraging such an improvisational climate is one of the leader's most important roles.

KEEPING IT LOOSE: BUILDING AN IMPROVISATIONAL CULTURE

Effective leaders make sure that systems like the ones we have described are in place to encourage the emergence of new strategies. Lars Kolind is President of a Danish hearing aid manufacturer, Oticon. In 1993 Oticon's sales grew 23 percent in a declining market; gross profit grew by 25 percent. He describes the leader's role in designing the systems that mean success:

> I don't see myself as a captain who steers the ship. I see myself as a naval architect who designs the ship. . . . It is more important to design the organization to act in a clever and responsible way than to control every action.

But building a culture that is comfortable with improvisation requires more than systems; it requires a mindset that celebrates unforeseen events, that looks at changing circumstances as opportunities rather than annoyances. That attitude needs to be modeled by the organization's leaders in order for evolving strategies to be valued and used. Kolind practices such flexibility:

As opportunities emerge, we see them and we act. Although Oticon has a budget and a strategic plan, we're not taking them very seriously. We're looking at long-term and short-term opportunities in a much more organic and dynamic way.[8]

Amar Bhide, a management writer, eloquently summarized the assumptions behind this critical leadership philosophy: "Businesses characterized by ease of entry, fast action, and service intensity are like poker, not chess. You play each hand as it is dealt and quickly vary tactics to suit conditions."[9]

In short, then, leaders need to provide the structure for improvisational strategy-making—the systems that allow strategies to emerge. They also need to demonstrate personally that responsiveness and flexibility are organizational values and *the* way to succeed in evolving markets. Only when those factors come together can evolving strategies truly provide a new and renewable source of competitive advantage.

While the organization's top leaders must set the tone and establish the structure that allows for wider participation in strategy-making, everyone in the organization has a critical role to play. In Part Two, we'll outline the various roles of leaders at all levels in the process, and provide examples of how companies are encouraging a new kind of strategist to make a significant contribution.

PART TWO

The New Strategists

6

The Role of the
Front-line Strategist

*Who will argue that only public men and corporation heads are entitled to have their
names emblazoned on the scroll of honor? . . . Workers are made of exactly the same stuff
as generals or presidents or governors or industrial leaders.*
                                                        —B.C. Forbes[1]

In 1988 a group of junior managers at Chrysler suggested that the corporation undertake an in-depth study of one of its key competitors, Honda.
Thanks to a 1987 speech by a Honda executive, they learned about
Honda's SED system. "S, or sales, comes up with the image of a new
product through discussions with customers," Shoichiro Irimajiri had
said. "Research and development—D—creates the specific design which
realizes the sales image. Production and engineering—E—find the way
to build the design. None of these groups does its work alone."[2]

The study, initiated by people far from the senior executive level,
helped drive the decision to create Chrysler's "platform teams," cross-
functional groups of designers, engineers, and executives who cooperated
at every stage of the development of the Neon car. "Chrysler's turnaround," *The Economist* noted recently, "resulted not from a grand corpo-

rate strategy handed down from on high, but from top management's decision to employ the wisdom already embedded in the organization."[3]

The quality and empowerment movements have been instrumental in helping organizations employ the wisdom of all their members to solve problems and identify opportunities for improvement. Success stories are plentiful and impressive. For example, at AT&T's Transmission Systems Business Unit, a 1992 Baldrige Award winner, a group of secretaries formed a team, on their own initiative, to tackle a problem that was interfering with their ability to be efficient and effective. They realized they were spending too much of their time and effort dealing with faxes that came in over the company's thermal fax machines. When a fax came in, the paper rolled; over time, the fax faded, so it needed to be copied, creating double the volume of paper for recycling. They felt that the entire process needed to be overhauled.

The most obvious solution was to change from thermal paper fax machines to plain paper ones. Replacing every fax machine in the facility would cost approximately $100,000. But the team was not to be deterred. They discovered and documented the savings of making such a shift: savings on the costs of recycling, thermal fax paper, copy machines, and time were much greater than the investment be required.

Louis Monteforte, Quality Planning Director for Transmission Systems, was impressed with the results: "It saved us half a million dollars by the time they got finished. I mean they were doing future value of money analysis, cash flow, and all this type of unbelievable stuff from quote/unquote 'a bunch of secretaries.'"

That example illustrates the power of leaders at all levels to help solve problems and uncover improvement opportunities. But their contribution doesn't have to be limited to improvement projects. They also have a critical role to play in gathering the information needed for strategy-making and in developing the cross-functional relationships that are so vital to the successful formulation and implementation of strategy. The front-line strategist may play the most important role in the strategy process—and the most overlooked one.

Who are these front-line strategists? As in the example above, they can indeed be secretaries; they can also be researchers, salespeople, customer service representatives, computer programmers, billing clerks, truck drivers, and manufacturing workers. They are the people who have direct contact with the business's customers and markets, who see on a daily basis what competitors are doing, and who understand how the key elements of the organization (for example, distribution or manufacturing) are working. They are the people whose work provides valuable information about the likelihood of the success of the strategies and the underlying assumptions they are based on. They are an organization's most valuable—and probably its untapped—source of strategic advantage.

Do front-line people in your organization see themselves as an integral part of your strategy process? Do they help others in the organization see how your strategies are playing out in the eyes of your customers? Are they actively seeking out information on new competitors and markets? Are they raising a red flag when a strategy or policy is *not* working? Essentially, front-line strategists have three principal roles to play in the strategy-making process:

- *Voice of the customer,* bringing the customer's viewpoint into the organization clearly and relentlessly
- *Hunter/gatherer,* actively seeking out information on competitors and markets to ensure that the unit's strategies are both focused on the most promising opportunities and responsive to new developments
- *Cross-functional magnet,* working effectively with people in other units and functions of the organization to provide the "magnet" that holds the business together in the service of your customers

Of course, senior executives should be doing these things as well. But if these functions aren't being performed by people on the front lines, it's virtually impossible to get the information you need about your customers and markets in order to formulate effective strategy. Let's look at each role in more detail.

VOICE OF THE CUSTOMER

Maybe you've had an experience similar to the one we had recently. We went into our neighborhood CVS store to buy cases of formula for our young son, Jack. As usual, we were in a hurry. We went to the place where the formula is kept but found only an empty shelf with a hand-lettered sign: "Cases of formula are now behind the register." We waited for five minutes in the register line. When it was our turn, the cashier informed us that they didn't have our brand behind the counter. She'd have to get it from the back of the store. Five minutes more. She came out with the wrong kind. Five minutes later, the right cases were brought to the register.

"Gee," we said, "this is really inconvenient. Maybe you could tell the manager about our concern—we buy a lot of formula here." "Oh," the cashier replied, "they tell us we have to do it this way, because a lot of formula was being stolen. We can't do anything about it." We left feeling certain that our request would never be relayed to anyone. We began buying formula at a different store. It's not a big deal to us. But it's no exaggeration to say that CVS lost several hundred dollars a month of our business (formula is expensive!).

Now, we could have asked to speak with the manager directly or filled out a customer comment card. But we didn't take the time to do that. And we shouldn't have to. Your customers—most of them—won't either. In a recent survey, the American Society for Quality Control listed the main reasons why companies lose customers. The number one reason, cited by 68 percent of the respondents, was that they were "turned away by an attitude of indifference on the part of a company employee." By comparison, only 14 percent left because they were dissatisfied with a product, and only 9 percent reported being lured away by the competition.[4]

The point is that the people in your organization who deal with the customer every day know what your customers want. They know what problems are arising and what people like and don't like about your products and the way you do business. Businesses often call these people customer service representatives. Too often, however, they see their role as *representing the company to the customer* —explaining, when they can, what the policies are. While this is certainly one aspect of their responsibilities, the other part of the equation is often left out. Their role is also *representing the customer to the company.*

Think, for example, about the difference between what happened to us at CVS and what might have happened if the cashier had responded instead with "Yes, I know it's inconvenient. . . . I'll talk with the store manager about it. I'm not sure that we can change the policy, but I'll call to let you know how we're going to address your concern."

Admittedly, there is a delicate balance to be achieved. It's important to avoid an "us versus them" mentality in any form. You certainly can't afford to have customers feel that the company is antagonistic toward them. Nor, on the other hand, do you want to set up a situation in which the front-line employee and the customer are allied against "company policy." The appropriate balance can be found only when the customer contact person represents both the needs of the business and the needs of the customer.

Finding ways to achieve this balance may mean substantial changes in the way you operate. The trend toward empowering front-line employees has implications for most of the systems your company has in place. Selection of new employees, for example, takes on increased importance. Companies like Disney and Marriott Hotels are overhauling their selection process to ensure that they find the right people for these critical customer contact jobs. "We used to hire people who were good at the keyboard, good at processing information," a Marriott human resources executive, Richard Bell-Irving, recounts. "Now we want associates who can look you in the eye, carry on a conversation, and work well under stress."[5]

Training also takes on increased importance. At Ritz-Carlton, employees receive training in the company's three steps of service—provide a warm greeting, anticipate or comply with guest wishes, and give a fond farewell. But, according to Vice President Patrick Mene, they are also taught that "within that process, it is their right to break away from their routine and apply some immediate positive action."

Front-line people need the encouragement, the skills, and the authority to represent your customers to the company. The company also needs to have systems in place to use the information gathered by your customer contact representatives.

At AT&T's Universal Card Services, a "customer comments platform" encourages associates to pass on any customer comments they receive. Greg Swindell, Chief Quality Officer, notes: "We really manage this like we would a request from a customer, but this is a request from the associate. We'll respond back to each and every individual so that they are more educated the next time a customer calls in. Then we also create communication vehicles that go back to *all* of our associates, communicating about that important issue."

Each month, management identifies the top ten themes from the customer comments. Swindell says, "The first thing we always talk about is 'What are the top ten things our associates are talking about?' And if I went down that list over time, I can tell you that just about every single one of those we have addressed in the marketplace. We're very focused on acting upon the information that we receive."

For example, front-line associates had frequently relayed customer requests for a rewards program. Some of them gathered information on the topic and spoke to customers about the kind of program they would like most. In 1994 Universal Card Services unveiled its "Something Extra" program to address this customer request. Swindell believes that this focus on listening and action is key to the business's phenomenal success.

Compensation is another piece of the puzzle. At Cadet Uniform Services, drivers, who are known as customer service representatives, manage their own routes and are responsible for their own accounts. Cadet ties compensation for these employees almost entirely to customer satisfaction. As a result, effective customer service representatives can earn upwards of $40,000 per year. "So many companies tell you how important their customers are," CEO Quentin Wahl says, "but hardly anyone actually pays their employees for satisfying them."[6]

HUNTER/GATHERER

Even when you have consistent and effective systems in place for representing customer views, you are only tapping the ideas and opinions of one part of your potential market, the people who are currently buying from you. It's equally important, strategically, to have people at all levels who are in tune with events in your markets, who know what competitors are doing and what trends are emerging.

The information-gathering role, which we call the "hunter/gatherer" and which has been called "external monitoring" by academics, has traditionally been ascribed to top management. However, just as people on the front line have a more direct and immediate pipeline to customers, they often have the most relevant and timely information about your markets and competitors. What they often don't have—and this is a critical distinction—are the skills to interpret which information is strategically important to the business and the encouragement to gather such information and share it with others in the organization.

At least initially, it can be helpful if senior management or unit leaders focus the information-gathering activities for a team or individual on a specific area.

Research on effective managerial practices[7] (which in a more participatory organization are used not only by managers but by leaders at all levels) suggests some relevant targets for information-gathering:

• *Who are our primary competitors, and what strategies do they appear to be pursuing in terms of pricing, advertising, and promotions; new products; and customer service?* People in the marketing function traditionally gather such trend data in a formal way, but others also can make valuable contributions. Salespeople, researchers, and product managers are likely sources for this kind of information. Newspapers and other current periodicals can prove invaluable as you try to detect competitors' moves in terms of strategy, new products, and pricing.

• *How do competitors' products and services compare to ours?* If you sell products directly to consumers, your own employees may be buyers themselves. Try asking them what products they are buying from your competitors and why. A sales clerk in a retail store who gets five requests in a month for a product you don't sell and refers potential customers to another store three doors down possesses critical strategic information, too. Commissioning a formal study of competitors' strengths and weaknesses, as Chrysler managers did with their Honda task force, can be a fertile source of new information as well.

• *Are events occurring that are likely to affect our current and potential external suppliers?* Your purchasing department should be on the lookout for such information, but so should others with critical ties to suppliers. When a shipping clerk hears from a UPS delivery person that UPS may go on strike next week, that information could have important consequences. When a manufacturing professional is the first to get wind of a shortage or a price increase on a component you buy from the outside, she becomes a front-line strategist by recognizing the importance of that information and taking the initiative to raise a red flag.

• *What is happening within government agencies and other regulatory organizations that could affect our business?* In an increasingly global business environment, government regulation—always a difficult factor strategically—becomes even more bothersome. If you are dealing with multiple governments, particularly ones that are unstable, the insights of your people on site become even more critical.

• *What changes are occurring in the kinds of technology we use to do business?* In high-tech industries, this question is the essence of strategic positioning. Even in low-tech industries, it is becoming increasingly important. If you are in the grocery business and the supermarket down the street is stealing your customers because they have just installed cash registers that accept charge cards, you need to know that in order to compete effectively.

In addition, several relevant areas outside your own industry and field should be watched closely by specific teams. They include shifts in demographics among the general population, economic trends, international political developments, and such cultural trends as increasing diversity in the workforce.

It is equally important to evaluate periodically the relevance of various types of information. Collecting too much information is costly and can be overwhelming for people who are trying to make sense of it. One of the leader's most important jobs, therefore, is deciding the kind of information that needs to be gathered by front-line people and developing a screening process that allows the most critical data to be incorporated into the business's plans.

In order to gather new ideas from customers and markets, people need to get away from their desks and actually go out into the world. At Rubbermaid, product development teams make a point of looking for new product ideas out in the field. For example, members of the commercial food team, which develops products for restaurant use, spend weeks working in their customers' kitchens. Industry trade shows and even museum exhibits are also fertile ground for new ideas.[8] Meetings with major current customers can prompt the identification of valued innovations to your products and services and opportunities to develop new ones. Chaparral Steel, which boasts the world's fastest per ton production time, has a compulsory annual education leave program. Employees visit customers, other companies, and universities to learn about innovative processes and technologies.[9]

When front-line workers see their role as the hunters and gatherers of information, creative ideas bubble up through the organization constantly and consistently. These people are, after all, experts in their respective fields, and their knowledge should be leveraged. It's not merely a matter of making them feel included. It's a great opportunity that can help your business stay on the leading edge of your industry.

CROSS-FUNCTIONAL MAGNET

In the pursuit of innovation, improvement, and customer focus, more and more front-line people are being organized into cross-functional teams in order to break down the "chimneys" of hierarchical and functionally driven organizations. Organizations are realizing that success in strategy depends on the ability of their various internal functions to work together. After all, those dotted lines on the organizational chart are only abstractions; it's the way that people throughout the business forge alliances to work toward a common goal that affects the success or failure of your strategies.

Cross-functional teams are an important vehicle for encouraging this kind of cooperation. In 1993, 86 percent of the 165 manufacturing executives we surveyed reported that the people in their businesses work in cross-functional teams more than they used to; 73 percent of the insurance industry executives we surveyed agreed.

While top management teams, by their very nature, have always been cross-functional in their composition, organizations now are creating cross-functional groups at all levels. At GE Capital Corporation, for example, sourcing teams are made up of people from a variety of functions. The teams have the responsibility for, among other things, managing the company's supplier relationships and negotiations. Product development teams at many companies (like the platform development teams at Chrysler) are cross-functional in composition from the very beginning of the process, in order to speed time to market and increase the likelihood of new product success by incorporating a broader spectrum of views and ideas.

Yet, while the use of cross-functional teams has mushroomed, the people in our survey indicated that the problem of how to coordinate effectively across functions is a long way from being solved. 93 percent felt that their organizations still need to improve teamwork and collaboration across functions in order to achieve their strategic goals, and 91 percent said that lack of communication between functions is having a negative impact on productivity.

Clearly, we still have a way to go in breaking down the walls between business functions. What's getting in the way? Interestingly enough, the usual suspect—the organizational structure—seems not to be the direct cause. When we asked people to react to the statement, "The structure of our company does not allow groups from various functions to interact easily," only 35 percent agreed. Obviously, there are other barriers to true cross-functional collaboration. While businesses may have put the teams in place to improve coordination between functions, the supporting systems and skills are not always there to help team members work together well. Essentially, the rules of the game are changing, and team members are just beginning to understand how to succeed in their new roles.

To find out more about the barriers team members are facing, we asked people what interfered with the effectiveness of cross-functional teams they had been a part of. These were some of the key barriers they cited:

• *Conflicting organizational goals (79 percent).* Team members often don't know how to resolve conflicts between the goals of their functions and the goals of the cross-functional team. When different functions are rewarded only for achieving their own internally driven goals, cross-functional conflict is inevitable.

• *Lack of clear direction/priorities (60 percent);* Team members don't always have a clear sense of what the team is expected to accomplish. Too often, teams are seen as an end in themselves, as a way to increase employee involvement. Organizations may focus on ways to get teams to operate effectively or on training in team processes, but those well-intentioned efforts are meaningless unless people know why the team was convened in the first place. Without clear goals, team initiatives often flounder.

• *Competition for resources (72 percent).* Many cross-functional efforts are under-resourced in terms of funding and, especially, in terms of the time team members have to devote to these projects. Becoming a team member too often involves taking on additional work and responsibilities with no respite from the other tasks of the formal job. As a result, team members can be forced to short-change their new assignment, particularly if it does not affect their performance evaluation and compensation in their "real jobs."

• *Overlapping responsibilities (70 percent).* Team members are often confused about their roles: Are they on the team to represent and fight for the views of their own functions, or should they work to find the best solution to an issue regardless of the impact on their specific area? How much authority do they have to make decisions and compromises that affect their units?

At times, middle managers, who may feel threatened by the emerging power of cross-functional teams, try to defuse their power by insisting that team members refer to them for all decisions. 3M's Robert Hershock recounts such an incident: "There was one member of the Operating Committee who was totally opposed to the change. And what he was doing was telling his people on the teams, 'You can go to the meetings, but you report back to me. Don't commit to anything, and you report back to me everything that was said.'"

Our survey results suggest that cross-functional team members are often caught in the middle of a kind of corporate tug-of-war. Team members may begin to feel like the mythical pushmi-pullyu from the Dr. Dolittle children's tales: a creature with two heads that share the same body. Demands from the function compete with the goals and responsibilities of the team, and progress is impeded. It's no wonder that another animal in the story asks: "How does it make up its mind?"

It seems that while teams have been created that bring front-line strategists together from different functions, many of the inherent conflicts between those functions have not disappeared, and they probably won't. After all, excellence in a specialized area often has a downside for another function. Pursuit of efficiencies and superb quality control in manufacturing operations may, for example, limit availability of equipment for product development testing. A salesperson's desire to respond to special customer needs may be at odds with other priorities in Operations or R&D. Even after reengineering—the 1990s answer to these problems—demands of one core process can infringe on the ability to maximize the efficiency of another.

What is needed then, is an organizational mindset that encourages people in various functions to balance the conflicting demands, priorities, and resource requirements that they will inevitably be faced with. Only then will companies be able to realize the strategic benefits they seek from organizing front-line employees into cross-functional teams. And only then will team members be able to fulfill their important role as the magnet that holds the various components of the organization together in the service of its customers.

BEGIN WITH SELF-EVALUATION

As a leader, you may want to ask people in your organization to read this chapter and evaluate their own behavior as front-line strategists, using the questionnaires in Appendix A. It's a critical role, and one that people may not be used to fulfilling. They will need your guidance and your encouragement as they take on new responsibilities and challenges. It's not an easy transition for many, but the payoffs are considerable—a better read on your customers' perceptions, a more observant eye on your market and industry, and improved cooperation across functions in the evolution of strategy.

7

The Strategy Integrator
The Role of the "Manager"

The test of a first-rate intelligence is the ability to hold two opposed ideas in the mind at the same time and still retain the ability to function.
—F. Scott Fitzgerald[1]

Bruce Dovey, a middle manager at The Geon Company, was concerned. He had established a team of people who reported to him and asked them to come up with a proposal for a big piece of plastic compound business for a major client. The team had developed an innovative approach to respond to the needs of this worldwide customer. The proposal included a number of servicing options and other value-added features that were not typical for this kind of product (which had traditionally been considered somewhat of a commodity). The customer liked the proposal, but asked Geon to lower the price. A competitor had submitted a lower bid based on less complex products and servicing options; the bid was below break-even margins for Geon and the industry overall. The customer wanted Geon to match that price. The team recommended that the company do so in order to get the business.

Dovey's boss, however, vetoed the team's decision to drop the price. While Geon's strategy was indeed to be a low-cost producer, he said, that did not mean holding onto market share at any cost. If the customer wanted the more specialized package, he would have to pay for it. Now Dovey faced the unenviable situation of having to go back to his team members and tell them that their decision had been overruled. He felt caught in the middle: How were team members going to feel empowered when their decisions were overturned? How were top managers going to learn to trust the team's decisions when they felt that the reasoning was not strategically sound?

Dovey's dilemma is one that is faced by middle managers every day in corporate life. James Autry, author of *Life and Work,* describes the competing demands placed on these leaders: "A leader must . . . inspire and often direct people in accomplishing the vision and mission and purpose of the organization while empowering people to manage themselves and make their own decisions."[2]

The leaders in the middle of organizations often know they need to cede some of their power so that people at all levels can make a meaningful contribution. As the Geon example illustrates, however, that is very difficult unless people in the unit understand the organization's strategic direction and the implications of those strategies for their own actions.

Of all the players in the strategy-making process, middle managers may face the most thorny challenges. In their daily dealings with customers, they too serve as front-line strategists, and need to fulfill most of the roles discussed in the previous chapter. And because they are the leaders of their own organizations, they face many of the same demands that corporate leaders face.

Most important, these men and women act as "strategy integrators," the link between different units and functions and between corporate leadership and the rest of the organization. That linkage is absolutely critical for the integration of strategy and action. Without it, even the best strategic plans will simply sit on the shelf. A former IBM marketing executive suggested that IBM's problems in the early 1990s were the result of just such a disconnection:

> What toppled IBM was not lack of strategic vision, but a failure to execute and follow through on strategy. . . . Back in the early 1980s, IBM manage-

ment put together a well-thought-out game plan . . . but somehow down on the field, no one was calling the signals. . . . Down in the divisions, regions and branch offices, the places where the "Awesome Strategy" really had to work, we went right on doing what we'd always done.[3]

The organization's ability to translate strategy into action is a direct result of the actions of its middle managers or strategy integrators. The scope of their responsibility varies widely from company to company, depending on the size and structure of the firm. In general, these people are at least one level below the corporate leadership of the enterprise; in a large corporation, they may have multiple levels between them and top management. They often have significant responsibility for both creating and carrying out strategies for their units (which are generally divisions, functions, or even small business units within a larger organization).

People in this role used to be called middle managers; in some businesses they still are. However, more and more companies are moving away from the use of the word "manager" entirely, because they feel that it connotes a command-and-control mentality they are trying to leave behind. AT&T's Global Information Solutions has done away with most of the titles in the organization. Even the CEO is now referred to as the "head coach." Craig Lotz, an AT&T coach, says, "We are trying to get away from 'I'm the manager, I'm the assistant vice president and you're the subordinate so you do what I say' and function more in a team environment."

Lotz describes his role as "coaching my associates and helping us be successful by encouraging, motivating, and providing resources, not by dictating, demanding, or instructing as to how things are accomplished." Even in companies that still give people at this level the title of "manager," the emphasis is often less on managing in the traditional sense and more on integrating the work of the various teams and individuals in the unit and making sure that people have what they need to operate effectively.

We call these people strategy integrators because they are responsible for ensuring that strategies developed at all levels of the organization are well integrated, while at the same time keeping the strategies flexible enough to respond to the specific needs of markets and customers. They, like people in other roles in the business, are also strategy-makers, but the coordination role is their most critical contribution to the process.

Strategy integrators have three principal roles:

• *Ambassadors.* Their job is to interpret the overall strategic direction set by corporate leadership and ensure that everyone in the unit understands the direction and its implications for them. In addition, they carry vital information and decisions back to senior executives and act as an advocate for strategies created in the unit. Finally, they often coordinate the strategies that have been created in diverse businesses and functions at their own level of the organization.

• *Facilitators.* They set up the process their units will use to evaluate diverse opportunities and strategic options and decide which will be pursued. This role requires a careful evaluation of the kinds of decisions that need to be made and the optimal way to involve people at all levels in the process.

• *Jugglers.* Effective strategy integrators find ways to juggle the diverse demands associated with both leadership and management. Although recent business literature cries out for more leaders and fewer managers, both leadership and management are important for strategic success.

AMBASSADOR

Strategy integrators often feel that they are caught in the middle—between corporate leadership and other employees in the organization—and, in fact, they are. They are the most obvious link in the chain between the entity's overall strategic direction and the various plans and goals developed in the specific businesses and functions. They thus become "ambassadors," representing their units to the leaders of the overall enterprise, and vice versa. That is often a difficult role, but it is an increasingly important one.

As greater responsibility is given to operating units for making their own strategies, strategy integrators in the middle of the organization become more and more critical to the business's strategic success. They interpret the overall strategic direction set by corporate leadership and help people in the unit understand what that direction means in terms of their daily actions. For that reason, strategy integrators themselves must have a very clear understanding of the strategic direction and the reasons behind it.

In our experience, there is often a great disparity between what middle managers actually know about a company's strategic direction and what top management thinks they know. An executive at a large insurance company that was implementing a major strategic shift noted, "It was a considerable surprise to discover how—to paraphrase Winston Churchill—so few knew so little about so much."

Strategy integrators can develop the required in-depth understanding only if they are actually made part of the strategy development process as it unfolds. Their involvement can take many forms. Undeniably, they need to be intimately involved in the development of formal strategies for their own units. The days when corporate planners dictated the strategies to line managers may not be gone entirely, but they are certainly numbered. Planners and corporate staff can serve a useful function—providing information, suggesting a proven process for planning—but they cannot have the depth of specific information and experience necessary to devise meaningful plans for each business unit. That can be done only by people with hands-on, daily contact with the markets they serve.

In addition, strategy integrators need the understanding and perspectives that stem from personal involvement with the development of strategies for the overall entity. That is because the overarching strategic direction establishes the context for the strategies of each business or function. Conferences and working sessions that include members of the "leadership group," rather than the top management team alone, are critical.

Such leadership group conferences not only serve to educate strategy integrators about the current direction but can provide excellent opportunities to identify and solve potential problems related to the implementation and likely success of strategies under consideration. The Canadian Imperial Bank of Commerce and General Motors' Chevrolet Division asked their leadership groups to identify possible barriers that could block successful implementation. They then organized the groups into teams to find ways to overcome the roadblocks or to suggest revisions to the strategy that would address the issues they had identified.

This kind of open debate and problem-solving also helps strategy integrators to understand how their units are connected to the whole. By talking with their colleagues in other functions, they are reminded of the interrelatedness of the various pieces of the business. They gain a clearer comprehension of how their own units' strategies affect and are affected by the work of other groups in the organization.

Understanding the current strategy is only the first step. The role of ambassador also requires expert communication skills and the utmost diplomacy. Communicating effectively to corporate leadership about the unit's strategies involves making a clear and compelling case for the proposed approach and for new strategies that are evolving. Effective communication to people in the unit involves not only a clear and straightforward description of *what* the overall strategic direction is, it means explaining the *why* behind the strategies being pursued and the changes they necessitate.

WEARING TWO HATS: COMMUNICATING WITH CORPORATE LEADERSHIP

In their dealings with corporate leadership (the senior executives who have the ultimate responsibility for guiding and integrating the elements of the overall enterprise), strategy integrators have two roles to play. First, they represent the needs, views, and strategies of their units. Second, they act as advisers who consider the good of the overall organization, evaluating actions and decisions in light of the total entity. AT&T's CEO, Robert Allen, puts it this way: "I ask the leadership team to wear two hats. I say, 'Come to our management meetings and represent your businesses. But there are going to be times when I ask you to put on *my* hat on behalf of the shareowners and help me make decisions that cross business-unit boundaries.'"[4] Xerox's Paul Allaire articulates a similar philosophy: "We want people who can hold two things in their heads at the same time, who can think in terms of their individual organizations but also in terms of the company as a whole."[5] Neither of these roles— the adviser for the entire organization or the advocate for an individual business—can be overlooked.

It is no secret that many large corporations have been bogged down by the warring of internal factions. Union Carbide languished at the back of the pack of chemical companies for twenty-five years, as it watched once smaller companies exceed UCC's growth and supersede it on the Fortune 500 list. Meanwhile, Union Carbide's various chemical divisions, battery and other consumer products groups, gas products businesses, and carbon electrode businesses fought fiercely among themselves for a bigger share of the corporation's resources. They expended more energy competing with other functions than they did fighting their true competition. Only since the breakup and sell-off of its non-chemical-related businesses has UCC finally begun to prosper along with its more focused competitors.

While other large corporations, most recently ABB, have found strategic success with a broad portfolio of individual businesses, Union Carbide never discovered a way to focus the energies of its diverse units on challenges of the external environment instead of on internal power struggles.

On the other hand, in the quest for cross-business cooperation, the importance of the other side of this dynamic cannot be forgotten. There is still much to be gained from bringing divergent views of different businesses and functions to the strategy table. After all, Marketing *should* be asking for new products; Manufacturing *should* be looking to optimize production efficiencies. Those divergent viewpoints can be used effectively, however, only if the overall strategic direction provides parameters and focus for the entire organization. For example, if a company's goal is to become the low-cost producer, R&D activities must focus on reducing the cost of operations and developing products that the company can market, not on doing costly basic research. In order for the diverse perspectives of the individual functions to be of value, they need to be put in the context of the strategies for the organization as a whole.

HEADS AND HEARTS: COMMUNICATING WITH PEOPLE IN THE UNIT

No matter how participatory the strategy process, there are times when a final decision must be made to clarify and codify an organization's strategic direction. That role is most often filled by the corporate leadership—the top management team and the leadership group. Most often, the strategic direction clarifies the organization's overall purpose, the kinds of products and services the company will offer to whom, and the relative importance of the various aspects of the corporate portfolio. And it describes, in a very basic way, how the entity will do business: which values and approaches form the foundation for strategic success.

Once the overall strategic direction has been clarified, the role of the strategy integrator is to convince others that the direction is the right one, that it will help the business succeed in the future, that it is the best among the possible alternatives, and that it is supported by facts, evidence, and logic.

Even before the current emphasis on empowerment, people have always wanted to know the "why" behind decisions and changes. Explaining not only "what" but "why" helps break down the barriers between corporate leadership and everyone else in the organization. Understanding the factors that went into a decision also helps people at all levels develop their own strategic thinking skills. Of course, it takes more time to explain the reasons behind a strategic decision rather than just announce it, but it is a critical aspect of being a leader whom people are eager to follow.

Robert Hershock at 3M described the enormous communication challenges involved with a major strategic shift for his division in the early 1980s:

> I had breakfast meetings and I'd invite about eight or ten different people a couple of times a week and try to explain to them what the issues were and why we were going to change, and how we were going to change. And then I took the Operating Committee with me and we went to each of the factories, and we met with every shift worker. We were there at 11:30 at night and we were there at 5:30 in the morning. We explained what the problems were and why we had to change, and what it meant to them. And even with all that, it's very, very difficult to change an organization.

To be effective, communication of strategies and standards cannot be a one-time event. As AT&T's Louis Monteforte notes, "We're talking about years of effort. You don't just wake up one morning and go out and say, 'I want you involved in the business and the number one customer satisfier is _____. Go work on it.' Because everyone goes back to work and says, 'Aah, that guy just came in and gave a speech.'" Consultant Jean B. Keffeler agrees: "People have an insatiable need to hear what's going on and what it means to them. They need to hear it again and again before they believe it . . . Information voids will be filled by rumors and speculation unless they are preempted by open, credible and trustworthy communication."[6] Mark Twain may have said it most succinctly: "A lie can travel half way around the world while the truth is putting on its shoes."[7]

Besides providing the logical arguments that help people understand the need for the strategies being pursued, strategy integrators must also appeal to people's hearts and values. In order for new strategies to succeed, people not only have to comply with the necessary changes; they have to be truly committed to their success.

Our extensive research conducted over the past fifteen years indicates that the most effective managers do this by:

- *Inspiring*: appealing to people's values or emotions to generate enthusiasm for strategies and a true belief that they will create a better future for the company and the people who constitute it
- *Rewarding*: providing tangible rewards such as pay increases or promotions for people who demonstrate the skills, competencies and values needed for the success of the strategy
- *Recognizing*: giving praise and showing appreciation for effective performance, significant achievements, and special contributions in support of the strategies

Managers who inspire others develop enthusiasm and commitment to the organization's strategies by linking people's work to their needs (for example, the need to feel important and useful or to develop new skills) and their values (loyalty, self-fulfillment, humanitarianism). Inspiring is likely to be most important when the organization is in turmoil, when the work is difficult and discouraging, or when the business is pursuing a high-risk strategy, such as market penetration or the introduction of a new product. (See Chapter 10 for more information on inspiring.)

Recent business press articles suggest that younger people entering the workforce are asking for this kind of connection to their ideals more than their earlier counterparts did. While the evidence to support those conclusions has not been plentiful, there is a kind of face validity to the contention that many people need more than a sound logical argument to prompt their true commitment. Especially in the face of changes in our mutual expectations of "lifetime employment," the rewards of spending more than eight hours a day at work include, for many, a belief that the company is really making a difference in arenas that are important to them.

Another important aspect of inspiring is leading by example: encouraging people to greater efforts through your own dedication and courage. While the leader should never be viewed by people in the organization as the "lone hero," he or she can serve as a very positive and visible demonstration of the behaviors that are required for the success of the strategies.

People are also more likely to be committed to a strategy when they are rewarded for their contributions. Rewards involve tangible benefits. The most common are pay increases, bonuses, more interesting job assignments, and promotions. Other rewards may include increased autonomy, a more flexible work schedule, and access to corporate leadership or important clients. Jerre Stead, former "head coach" of AT&T's Global Information Solutions, maintains that "ninety percent of what people call cultural conflicts exist because of conflicts in measures and rewards."[8]

Rewards can send a powerful message about which behaviors, values, and skills are most needed in order for your organization to achieve its strategic goals. When you promote a person who prefers to make autocratic decisions, while at the same time espousing a new climate of involvement, the message you send is at best contradictory. The management writer Stephen Kerr calls this "the folly of rewarding A, while hoping for B."[9] Such folly occurs frequently, especially when strategic goals are changing. Changes in reward systems often lag far behind shifts in strategies, creating a discontinuity that frustrates management's best efforts to instill new behaviors and values.

In some organizations, middle managers have a great deal of power to provide tangible rewards; in others they have virtually none. Even if you have little control over rewards like pay and promotions, you can motivate people with something less tangible but often equally or more compelling: recognition. Recognizing involves complimenting people for unusual creativity, initiative, persistence, or skill, giving them credit for their ideas and suggestions, and acknowledging important achievements in a meeting or special event. Jerre Stead notes that "attaboys, letters, notes, trips . . . really pound out rewards."

Dan Wilkowsky, Director of Corporate Environmental and Safety Services for National Semiconductor, describes the company's "Breakfast for Champions" recognition program:

> The idea was that each site has some people who are doing good things from the environmental and safety standpoint; they are not necessarily the environmental professionals. Let's publicize their behaviors. So, that's what we've done. Each site essentially has one of these breakfasts, often with people from the press, and local leaders like the mayor and city council people. People get up and talk about what they or their team did, and they are given a plaque and maybe some money. We've been doing the Breakfasts for Champions for two years, and the program almost runs itself now.

National Semiconductor discovered the importance of rewarding teamwork, a key element required to fulfill its strategy, by benchmarking against other companies. Other regional rallies and forums, which they call "Pursuit of Excellence," bring teams together to share success stories with each other and with top management.

Being an ambassador, then, involves much more than being a messenger of information. As a representative of the unit, it means knowing which hat to wear when—when to be an advocate for the interests of the function or business and when to focus on the bigger picture. As a representative of corporate leadership, it means not only communicating the strategies in a clear and compelling way but also motivating people at every level to give their all to help the strategies succeed.

NEW AMBASSADORIAL CHALLENGES

What were once strictly vertical flows of information are being broken down. Middle managers, who were once virtually the only channel for information up and down the organizational chart, are often sharing this responsibility with others in their organizations. New processes and structures are creating access to corporate leadership for employees at all levels.

An excellent example of the shift is provided by the 3M unit we have mentioned previously. In 1983, when the Occupational Health and Environmental Safety Division first chartered its new product development teams, it gave each team a senior management sponsor who also sat on the Operating Committee (the top management team of the division). "They didn't necessarily go to all the team meetings," Robert Hershock recalls, "but the sponsor was a person who could get the team resources, could solve problems."

"Now, an interesting thing happened," he continued, "when, all of a sudden, teams were connected to the Operating Committee through the bridge of the sponsor. Middle management was getting less and less information. They felt that they were out of the loop. They really started to question what their role was going to be."

This division addressed the middle management dilemma through training. ("We really did it backwards," Hershock admits. "We had to go back and train the middle management people and try to bring them into the process.") Middle managers were also brought into the process as members of the product development teams.

Other companies report a similar difficulty with the reactions of middle managers to new ways of working. Here are some representative quotes from the people we interviewed:

- "The real squeeze comes at middle management; they wonder, 'What am I going to do, what's my role in all of this?' Middle management has some real concern about how they are going to stay informed, but still allow the groups to perform autonomously."

- "We still see a little bit of resistance at the middle management level. They got to be middle managers by telling people what to do."
- "The struggle we faced and still face was in the upper middle level of the organization; these people really struggle with their loss of power and influence when teams are given a direct pipeline to top leadership."

These quotes highlight a critical shift in the role of ambassadors: In some organizations, new structures and processes are bypassing the middle manager, making a direct connection between senior management and front-line strategists. If you are a middle manager in such an organization, you need to find a way to contribute value by serving as a resource and by supporting the cross-functional teams with encouragement, rewards, and expertise. As with the other aspects of your role, which we'll describe in the rest of this chapter, part of the job is helping to develop the skills of others in your organization to perform tasks previously reserved for middle managers.

FACILITATOR

Another aspect of the strategy integrator's role is to facilitate the process by which people in the unit formulate strategies. This involves evaluating the numerous options and opportunities that are uncovered and deciding which will be adopted. Empowerment, after all, is not a blanket permission to pursue any action or strategy; there must be some way to coordinate the diverse efforts of the people in the unit in order to ensure that they are aligned with the organization's overall strategic direction.

As facilitators, strategy integrators share much of the work traditionally known as strategic planning. Planning can involve determining long-term objectives and strategies, allocating resources according to priorities, and determining how to improve coordination, productivity, and effectiveness. The strategy integrator, in essence, sets up the process for judging the merits of the various proposals and deciding which will be undertaken and which will not.

For example, a group of managers in the manufacturing function of UST's tobacco division developed a team-based process for strategic planning. They felt that they needed a way to get people in the organization aligned behind a set of common goals and focused on the future. The planning team they assembled involved the heads of the main functions with which manufacturing needed to coordinate. This cross-functional team identified key strategic issues and chartered other teams to act on them. The process was so successful that it eventually spread to every function in the tobacco division, and even to the company's entertainment and international divisions.

In an emergent way, the process began to involve people at lower levels in each function. "Directors would ask each other to be on their teams," Nick Amadori, the Director of Employee Relations who facilitated the sessions, reports. "Before long, they didn't have enough time to be on all the teams, so they would ask someone two or three levels down to represent their functions."

Notice that we're not saying that strategy integrators always make the final strategic decisions. They are, however, often responsible for deciding who will. Ralph Stayer, the celebrated CEO of Johnsonville Foods, puts it this way: "The strategic decision is who makes the decision."[10]

PARTICIPATORY DECISION-MAKING

Too often, decision-making is viewed as a kind of false dichotomy: Either you have a participatory culture in which groups make decisions, or you have an autocratic one in which the leader decides. In reality, the degree of participation in decision-making falls along a continuum. At the far left of this continuum, you'll find "group decision-making." Here the leader turns the decision-making power over to a group and has no more influence over the final outcome than any other member of the group. At the far right of the spectrum is "autocratic decision-making." The leader makes the decision alone, without asking for suggestions from others. In between the two extremes, however, is a wide band of "consultative decision-making," in which the leader invites, to varying degrees, the participation of others, yet reserves the right to make the final call.

How do you know which approach to use in setting up the strategy development process for your unit? Research shows that the success of a strategic decision depends on two things: the quality of the decision itself and its acceptance by those who will be affected.

Participation by other people will improve the quality of a decision only if they have relevant information, ideas, and skills. You are least likely to have a monopoly in these areas when the decision is complex—that is, when the cause of the problem is difficult to pinpoint, when the solution is not obvious, and when any choice requires some tradeoffs between potential benefits. Most strategic decisions fall into this category.

Regardless of how high the quality of a decision is, it will not be successful if people who are affected refuse to accept it. Participation in decision-making is one way of increasing people's acceptance of the result. When people have substantial influence over a decision, they tend to identify with it and come to regard it as "their" decision. They also gain a better understanding of the reasons behind the decision. When they have a chance to express their reservations about the possible consequences of a decision and can ask for specific changes and safeguards, their anxiety and resistance to change are likely to be lower. And, as we have pointed out in previous chapters, wider participation creates more opportunities for strategies to evolve and ultimately become part of formal strategic plans.

Despite the benefits of more participatory decision-making, there are times when an autocratic decision will actually be accepted. That is most likely to occur when:

- The course of action you choose just happens to be the one that people like
- People share your objectives, and you have the expertise and skill to persuade them that your decision is the best way to reach those goals
- They will support you out of loyalty and admiration, even though they may not agree with your decision
- There is a crisis, and people recognize the need for decisive leadership

In the modern organization, we would caution you that these conditions are more the exception than the rule. And you should be aware that your own perceptions of how frequently you are involving people at other levels may not match their own views. In a 1994 study, the Wyatt Company reported that 61 percent of senior managers felt that they did a good job of involving employees in decisions that affected them. However, two-thirds of the nonmanagerial people surveyed disagreed.[11]

In the same year a comprehensive Worker Representation and Participation Survey asked more than 2,500 people in nonmanagerial, supervisory, and middle management jobs how satisfied they were with the amount of influence they have on company decisions. Only 23 percent of nonmanagers and 30 percent of lower-level managers reported that they were "very satisfied." While 63 percent of all respondents reported that they wanted more influence on company decisions, only 6 percent felt that this was "very likely," with 22 percent answering "somewhat likely."[12] In their summary of the research findings, professors Richard Freeman and Joel Rogers report: "The vast majority of employees want more involvement and greater say in company decisions affecting their workplace. They believe increased influence will not only give them greater job satisfaction, but also improve the competitive performance of companies."[13]

Those results suggest that, more often than not, companies need to establish a process that relies on consultative decision-making. As a facilitator of the process, the strategy integrator has the difficult but indispensable task of determining how people will be involved in formal strategic decision-making. Is that process clear in your unit? Do people understand not only which decisions they are being asked to make, but which ones can be overruled? Do people in your unit have the knowledge and skills to improve the quality of the decisions they are a part of? Do you know how people feel about the process and their role in it?

Answering those questions requires the ability to juggle the sometimes competing demands of empowerment and coordination, of strategic flexibility and alignment. "At one extreme," James Howard, CEO of Northern States Power, observes, "you can send missives out of the corporate office every day. At the other, you can hold an employee referendum on the plaza every day. You have to find a happy medium."

JUGGLER

In fact, the really effective strategy integrator is probably most like a juggler, lofting several balls into the air at the same time and maintaining the momentum based on years of skill and experience. In addition to juggling the demands associated with their roles as ambassadors and facilitators, middle managers have to ensure that their units are performing efficiently and effectively. More than people in any other role, they must juggle the diverse demands of what we know as "leadership" and "management."

The leadership versus management debate has been a hot topic among those who provide advice to organizations. In the current *zeitgeist,* leadership is in and management is out. Here are some representative quotes from the leadership gurus:

- "The manager is a copy; the leader is an original. . . . The manager relies on control; the leader innovates. . . . The manager is the classic good soldier; the leader is his own person. The manager does things right; the leader does the right thing."[14]
- "We must come to grips with the nauseating possibility that most managers have added negative value to our corporations."[15]
- "We need less management and more leadership. . . . Management assumes controlling, directing, checking. . . . Leadership is a very different quality—it involves creating direction through vision, direction through inspiration, direction through example, as opposed to direction through control."[16]

Put that way, few people would argue that they would rather be managers than leaders. This is, however, a false dichotomy, and one that may be leading people in organizations astray. James Autry notes: "It's not as if a manager wakes up in the morning and says, 'Well, I've got to go be a leader today; I've got to enunciate a vision, walk around a bit, assure alignment, empower people and so on.' Nonsense."[17]

Certainly there is much to be said for encouraging people at all levels to develop qualities traditionally associated with leadership: focusing on long-term priorities and opportunities, inspiring others, reinforcing critical organizational values. These qualities are necessary but *not sufficient* for the business to function effectively.

However out of favor it may be currently, "management" is still a critical factor in an organization's strategic success. Research studies conducted over the past twenty years have identified practices used by effective managers.[18] These include such behaviors as clarifying (communicating a clear understanding of responsibilities, objectives, priorities, deadlines, and performance expectations), problem-solving (identifying problems, analyzing them in a systematic and timely manner, and acting decisively to implement solutions and resolve crises), and team-building (facilitating the constructive resolution of conflict and encouraging cooperation, teamwork, and identification with the unit). Which of those practices, we ask, can the organization do without?

Even the managerial practice of monitoring remains a critical part of a leader's job. Monitoring involves gathering information about work activities and external conditions affecting the work, checking on the progress and quality of the work, and evaluating the performance of individuals and the effectiveness of the unit. Those who contend that monitoring is a remnant of a bygone command-and-control era would do well to remember the Joseph Jett debacle at Kidder, Peabody & Co., which cost its parent company GE close to $400 million. For nearly two years, Jett, Kidder's chief government bond trader, allegedly manipulated its trading and accounting systems to generate millions in false profits. An internal analysis issued in August 1994 blamed Jett's supervisors for their lack of oversight and understanding of the trader's activities.

Empowerment, ironically, actually brings with it the need for *increased* monitoring on the part of management. People are taking on new roles and responsibilities, they are using new skills and working in new arenas. If managers are truly to be transformed from supervisors into coaches, how will they know what amount and kind of coaching is required without monitoring the work?

Admittedly, the word "monitoring" has some Big Brother–like connotations that are not consistent with the new workplace ethos. It needs to be done in a way that encourages people to take responsibility for the quality of their own work. It needs to be done in a consultative way, so that everyone has a say in what will be monitored, why, and how. But it still needs to be done.

So, to the argument that we need "more leaders and fewer managers," our reply is that management and leadership are work processes (not kinds of people) and that both are critical to the strategic success of any organization. We need more people at all levels engaged in the work of management and leadership, not an artificial distinction between the two. Organizations could make real progress by breaking the mindset that leads to labeling some people "managers" and others "leaders." Management and leadership are required of everyone in order to achieve shared goals.

Juggling the demands of both areas is particularly critical for people in the role of strategy integrator. They are leaders of their units in their own right. They are also ultimately responsible for the effective day-to-day functioning of their units, a role that requires some of the practices traditionally associated with management.

While a balance between these two perspectives is the ideal, obviously, some people will be more inclined toward the big picture perspective of the leader; others will be more comfortable with the procedures and systems that are so integral to effective management. It's important for people to play to their strengths as well as to develop new abilities. Therefore, the real goal is to ensure that the organization has a balanced cadre of people at all levels with strengths in each area. That, too, is the ultimate responsibility of the strategy integrator.

IN SUMMARY . . .

The strategy integrator's role—as ambassador, facilitator, and juggler—is fraught with potential difficulties, yet it is critical. Effectiveness in this role most often requires years of experience and great skill. In essence, it is the training ground for corporate leadership—but this role is not just a stepping stone to a senior management job. It is equally important for the strategic effectiveness of the business.

8

The Strategic Leader
The Role of the Senior Executive

No one is great enough or wise enough to surrender our destiny to. The only way in which anyone can lead us is to restore to us the belief in our own thinking.
—Henry Miller[1]

Because senior executives have long been seen as the strategy-makers in the organization, their role in the process has been the most extensively written about and examined. In fact, the frequent in-depth analysis of the challenges facing the leader at the top of the organization (and it is most often expressed that way—*the* leader, not *leaders*) may have a considerable and unconsidered downside. When we focus all our attention on the work and skills of the leader at the top of the organizational chart, we risk ignoring and minimizing the roles of the leaders at all levels who, cumulatively, can have more impact on the organization's actual strategy.

We are not suggesting, however, that executives have no role to play in the process of strategy-making. They do, of course, and it is a critical function that cannot be fulfilled by even very skilled and dedicated leaders at other levels. While our emphasis in this book is on giving rein and responsibility to new kinds of strategists, this focus comes from the

117

desire to highlight a shift in that direction and to respond to a historical imbalance, not to strip top managers of their indispensable role in the process.

Senior managers, as noted earlier, must do much more than simply select the right people and get out of the way. What the work actually involves has been delineated in a plethora of models, studies, theories, and exemplars presented by management theorists and the business press alike. To leaders and future leaders of organizations, the advice must seem cacophonous and, too often, more theoretical than practical.

What, for example, should a leader do differently when he is advised that his focus on organizational structure must be transformed into a focus on processes? That strategic planning is outdated, but communication of strategic intent is now required? That her job is to create stretch targets or a learning organization or a climate of "intrapreneurism"? While many of those notions, put forward in eloquent and often convincing detail by management writers, have useful and inspirational messages, too frequently they are embraced fully without adapting the proposed system or perspective to the needs and circumstances of the individual business. "There are not whole truths; all truths are half-truths," Alfred North Whitehead remarked. "It is trying to treat them as whole truths that plays the devil."

We do not believe, as others have contended, that the willingness to try new approaches and adopt new lexicons comes from top managers' desire for a quick fix to complex problems. ("Executives," one researcher notes, "have a never ending love affair with new programs and one-shot 'fix-its.'"[2]) Instead, we believe that the search for "an answer" most often springs from a very real and passionate desire to do what's best for the organization and from an admirable openness to new ideas and new ways of competing.

Business people, and senior executives in particular, are generally portrayed in the popular culture as greedy, lazy, rigidly bureaucratic, and heartless. If the view seems extreme, pay attention to the next five movies or television shows you watch that involve characters in a traditional business environment. Which of the characters are shown as ethical, hardworking, flexible, or compassionate? Virtually none are. The consistently sinister portrayals of top executives are not only generally inaccurate in our experience, they are a barrier that prevents open communication in the workplace. Overcoming such perceptions is one of the key challenges facing executives who would foster the open, give-and-take environment so necessary for effective strategy-making at all levels. In fact, many of the challenges confronting leaders in modern organizations fall into the general category of overcoming cynicism and battling false perceptions.

In their desire to move their organizations forward constructively, however, senior executives may indeed be seduced by perspectives that promise "the key." Rather than add, therefore, to the numerous and competing models and vocabularies that prescribe how to chart a successful course for an enterprise, we'll focus on what the most successful senior executives in a wide array of industries actually do and what characteristics they share.

The characteristics of effective strategic leaders can be best expressed through the metaphor of the tightrope walker, who needs focus, balance, and coordination to get from one end of the thin wire to the other. Those qualities cannot be learned in a one-week course; they cannot be taught through case studies. While they can be demonstrated and debated, they can be learned only through experience—experience gained through having the responsibility and challenges of leadership as early as possible in a career. This is yet another reason to distribute strategy-making power more widely; the leaders of tomorrow are, at this moment, learning the lessons and developing the capabilities they will need to help your business succeed in the future.

Like the tightrope walker, an effective strategic leader evinces three critical abilities: focus, balance, and coordination. In a business organization, those qualities mean:

- *Focus:* clarifying the organization's strategic direction and vision for the future
- *Balance:* helping people resolve dilemmas associated with the strategic focus and remain open to change
- *Coordination:* ensuring that the diverse functions and strategic ini-

tiatives of the organization work in harmony in the service of shared goals

FOCUS

Tightrope walkers keep their eyes on their ultimate destination, not on the inch of wire directly in front of them. At the same time, they pay un-wavering attention to adjusting their current position in order to stay aloft. In a similar way, effective corporate leaders spend a great deal of time looking forward, while maintaining an unwavering sense of the current strengths and weaknesses of the organization.

"Men and women with a knack for strategic planning are future-orient-ed and in particular they realize the reality of the future. . . . They realize what needs to be done now if benefits are to accrue in the future," the management expert Peter Vaill writes. "Yet for all their vision and ambi-tiousness, effective strategic thinkers have their projects grounded in the operational problems and opportunities of some particular organization. In this sense they are practical as well as visionary."[3]

Because many top leaders of corporations are delegating the responsi-bility for the development of specific strategies to leaders at other levels, they are looking to broader statements of corporate vision—portraits of future success—to provide the needed focus and alignment for their or-ganizations.

For simplicity's sake, we'll call the "portrait of future success" a vi-sion; your corporate terminology may call it something else. Organiza-tions and management writers have a wide array of labels for and definitions of the "vision thing." In fact, the semantic debate about the differences between statements of vision, mission, purpose, values, strategic intent, and so on may have actually obscured rather than clari-fied this vital leadership role.

What we call a vision is the expression of what the organization *needs to be and is capable of becoming* by a specific point in the future. The vi-sion is not a pie-in-the-sky wish list, nor is it a description of an organi-zation that is perfect in every imaginable way. It is a challenging but realistic picture of the business as it will be when current strategies have been realized. Using a point in the not-too-distant future, a vision describes what your organization will be doing for a living. It may also describe how you will stand in relation to your competitors, how your customers, suppliers, and associates will view you, and what you will stand for.

The primary purpose of such a vision is to focus the current efforts of the organization in a way that is catalyzing but not constraining. David A. Simon, Deputy Chairman at British Petroleum, describes the role of the company's statement of purpose: "It is not self-explanatory but is written in a way to promote conversation. . . . Its power lies in the outcome of those conversations and translations."[4]

"What has not been fully appreciated about 'the vision thing,'" James O'Toole and Warren Bennis write, "is that the purpose of a clearly communicated vision is to give meaning and alignment to the organization and, thus, to enhance the ability of *all* employees to make decisions and create change. The new leader does not make all decisions herself; rather, she removes the obstacles that prevent her followers from making effective decisions *themselves*."[5]

THE FAILURE OF VISION

Despite the important role a vision can play in focusing the work of people in an organization, efforts to create such a vision are prone to failure. Too often such efforts produce no more than a nicely framed statement on the wall; they fail to achieve their true purpose: inspiring changes in people's behavior that are consistent with the organization's strategy. John Rock, general manager of GM's Oldsmobile, recently said what many have been thinking about the irrelevance of some vision statements: "A bunch of guys take off their ties and coats, go into a motel room for three days, and put a bunch of friggin' words on a piece of paper—and then go back to business as usual."[6]

Visions fail to do what they are meant to do for several reasons:

- *Pitfall 1.* The vision is crafted by people at the top of the organization without sufficient input from others.

- *Pitfall 2.* The vision doesn't take the current reality of the organization into account.
- *Pitfall 3.* The vision is unconnected to action.
- *Pitfall 4.* The vision doesn't capture the true purpose and values of the organization.

PITFALL 1: VISION WITHOUT INCLUSION

When a vision is created at senior levels without sufficient input from people at other levels, even the best "communication" effort will rarely result in true commitment. If even middle managers feel removed from the process and the reasoning behind the vision of the company, how will a front-line customer service rep feel? If he has been excluded from the process and has little understanding of the reasons behind the vision, how likely is it that he will use the vision to drive his daily behavior and decisions?

Advice about the need for visionary leadership, like advice about strategy, is too often put in an individual context, implying that a lone leader comes up with a vision and, if he or she is effective, inspires others to follow it. Here are some representative viewpoints:

- "To be a good leader you have to have a clear vision of what you want to get done, and keep focused on that vision."[7]
- "The very essence of leadership is [that] you have to have a vision. It's got to be a vision you articulate clearly and forcefully on every occasion."[8]
- "Certainly a transforming leader—that is, a leader who is going to transform our reality—is one who has a vision, some notion of where he or she wants to go. . . . When vision is communicated to other people, it motivates them."[9]

Certainly, an organization's leaders need to *help* people develop a shared sense of what the organization stands for and where it is going. However, we contend that the most effective leaders *clarify and coalesce* the purpose and future direction for the organization. Some people and units in the organization are already heading in this direction; others may not be. Strategic leaders put the spotlight on the efforts and perspectives that are most important for future prosperity. The elements are usually already there, but leaders help people see them more clearly and focus on those that are most critical for success.

This view is at odds with the notion that *the* leader is all-knowing and envisions possibilities that no one else has considered. The popular conception of visionary leadership celebrates such individual genius. If that is the case in your organization, you might feel comforted and confident that you are working for such a brilliant, decisive individual. On the other hand, perhaps you should be asking, "What is preventing leaders at all levels from discovering these opportunities for themselves?"

The role of the leaders at the top of organizations, then, is not single-handedly to formulate a vision of the future so much as to identify and sift through the competing visions bubbling throughout the organization and to integrate them into a compelling and unifying portrait of future success.

The leadership group, which is generally composed of the top fifty to eighty managers in a large corporation and the top twenty or so in a smaller unit, should be responsible for clarifying and expressing a shared and achievable picture of the future of the entity. The task is infinitely more complex than coming up with a vision in one person's mind, but it is also much more likely to generate enthusiasm, true understanding of strategic focus, and commitment to achieving shared goals. "We have found, in practice," one CEO reports, "that people are much more effective in pursuing ideas that are their own than in trying to follow someone else's ideas."

A warning about asking people for their input into your organization's vision: William Moffett reminds leaders to "just ask the question, 'How serious am I about empowering employees at all levels in the company?' If there are limits to what management will accept, state those limits. . . . To do anything else is deceptive."[10]

PITFALL 2: YOU CAN'T GET THERE FROM HERE

Leaders who are crafting a vision often stumble because they place more emphasis on making the vision inspiring than on making it achievable.

Many visions fail what we call the "snicker test." That happens when people in an organization read a vision statement and respond not with heightened commitment but with a snicker. It happens because the vision (which may indeed be challenging and creative) is so far from the reality of the current business as to be almost laughable.

When a vision fails the snicker test, the process used to develop it is usually at fault. Conventional wisdom would say that you first develop a picture of what you want to be in the future; then you take stock of where you are; then you decide how to get from here to there (your strategies). We suggest reversing the process. An achievable and realistic vision can be crafted only after a detailed analysis of the current environment and competitive position of the business. While a vision describes the future, it must be grounded in the realities of today.

The vision statement sets some parameters that help senior managers decide which strategies will be pursued. However, in the same way that tactics often drive the strategy, the strategies themselves can affect the vision. When we work with strategy teams to help them craft a vision and codify their strategies, the process is iterative. They use a draft of the vision to help them identify strategic options that will get them from where they are now to where they want to be. But if those strategies are undoable given the organization's current strengths and market environment, or if they involve more risk than the business is willing to take, the team goes back and revises the vision.

That approach does not ignore the fact that organizations and people can often achieve the seemingly unachievable by being challenged to meet a "stretch target." "Stretch targets," according to *Fortune* magazine, "reflect a major shift in the thinking of top management. Executives are recognizing that incremental goals, however worthy, invite managers and workers to perform the same comfortable processes a little better every year."[11] Stretch targets, on the other hand, such as 3M's goal to generate 30 percent of revenue from new products, set challenging and specific goals in areas like product development time and inventory turns. They are not, however, a substitute for vision. They are a measurable way to make a vision into reality.

PITFALL 3: ALL VISION, NO ACTION

Stretch targets are being used to address another frequent failure of the visioning process: visions that are unconnected to action. "In organizations," Robert Eccles and Nitin Nohria say, "words without deeds are less than empty since they can potentially undermine the power of all the words that follow them."[12]

Vision statements are often viewed as "words without deeds" because they are too generic; that is, if you took the company name off the statement, it could represent virtually any business in any industry. In order to make the vision flexible enough to accommodate shifts in strategy, it is expressed in such general terms that it becomes almost meaningless. Here is where the tightrope act comes into play.

Crafting a vision that is both flexible enough to allow for evolving strategies and specific enough actually to mean something is no easy task, but it is an essential one. Lew Platt, CEO of Hewlett-Packard, puts it this way: "Senior management's role is *not* to tell business units what opportunity to take. Instead, our role is to create the environment that encourages business managers to take risks and create new growth opportunities. In other words, vision at HP isn't a straitjacket that constrains our managers, but rather a view of the many opportunities ahead."[13]

Because the vision itself should be concise enough to be easily recalled, it's helpful to translate it into more specific, measurable targets. Those targets or standards break the vision down into more manageable pieces and outline the things the organization must *do* in order to make the vision real. Standards can be used to provide shared objectives for the entire organization, monitor progress, measure achievement, identify key areas for improvement, and set performance goals.

For example, the 1993 vision statement of a corporate bank began with these sentences: "We are an innovative corporate bank built on strong relationships. We advise, structure, arrange and provide for all layers of capital by using our expertise in corporate finance and capital markets. We are a leader in the delivery of quality products and services to meet the critical financing needs of our customers."

That general statement on its own would be unlikely to generate much in the way of action. However, it was augmented by several of the business' standards:

- We increase the number of all customers who call us a principal bank by 20 percent per year.
- We are recognized as a leading financial services provider by the national industry groups we targeted in 1990.
- We are among the top ten providers in each product group, and we are among the top five in some product groups.

The bank's leadership group, with substantial input from others in the organization, identified ways to gather the information needed to measure progress on the key standards. They also asked people throughout the organization to generate ideas about how to meet the targets that had been identified. In this way, the vision was used to drive the selection of strategic projects and programs designed to achieve the goals. Although their vision statement, like those of many other companies, did hang on the walls of the bank's offices, it did much more. It inspired action and change.

PITFALL 4: THE VISION WITHOUT A HEART

The final reason for the frequent failure of the visioning process is that it treats the people in the organization as "resources" to be marshaled instead of recognizing them as people with hearts and values. Visions that focus on financial measures such as profitability often fail to engage people's emotions and commitment. They also overlook a basic human drive—the desire to make a difference. An effective vision includes words that describe the organization's fundamental purpose, which is the important societal need the organization fills. One manager put it this way: "It's fine to emphasize what we should shoot for, but we also need to know what we stand for."[14]

Leaders in the 1990s and beyond are recognizing the need to appeal to a higher purpose than simple profit-making. Goran Lindahl, an executive vice president at ABB, argues that "in the end, managers are loyal not to a particular boss or even to a company but to a set of values they believe in and find satisfying."[15]

Values and culture, as much as vision, are guiding principles that let people at all levels formulate consistent strategies on a day-to-day basis. "Our values give us an anchor at HP," CEO Lew Platt says. Those values, known as the HP way, include trust and respect for individuals, achievement, integrity, teamwork, flexibility, and innovation. "They are quite enduring. . . . But while we want continuity, we can't have stagnation. We need flexibility in order to adapt to a changing environment. So, while our values stay the same, our practices can—and must—change."[16]

Such values are conveyed first and foremost, through action. Which people are rewarded, promoted, celebrated? Which teams receive attention and respect? Which words become part of the corporate vocabulary? How does the company deal with suppliers, with customers, with its own people? More than any formal statement, those actions confirm the values of the organization.

George Hatsopoulos at Thermo Electron is clear about the values of his company and uses the recognition of people who embody those values to communicate them to others. "What matters in our organization," he says, "is results in terms of developing a product or business. And the more good that business does to society, the better that person gets recognized. The people we celebrate are the ones who helped develop an artificial heart that saved thousands of lives, or who developed a remediation technology that will help abate pollution."

Values can also be conveyed through written statements, although they are not always expressed in a separate document. They can be embedded in the vision and strategies of the organization. The corporate bank vision statement and standards cited earlier provide a good example of the integration of values and strategy. An excerpt from the vision statement reads this way: "Teamwork is our hallmark. We bring people together as partners to get the job done." This general statement is supplemented by one of the standards: "People are rewarded for demonstrating commitment to teamwork and to the overall partnership."

That standard, in turn, was backed up by changes in the performance appraisal process, which was revised to incorporate peer reviews, training programs that helped people build cross-functional teamwork skills, and new measurement systems that allowed the organization to track progress in increasing the levels of teamwork in the service of customers.

A CAVEAT ABOUT VALUE STATEMENTS

Like visions, however, statements of values often fail to make the transition from corporate dogma to real action. At a very large insurance company, for example, the Chairman spent a great deal of time and energy in the early 1990s emphasizing the enterprise's "Core Values." They were posted in the halls of every office. They adorned the coffee cups in the cafeteria. They were required elements of training programs.

Despite the large-scale and expensive communication effort, the core values did not, for many, pass the "snicker test." They seemed unconnected to the actions of the top leaders of the organization. "Who are they, driving around in their limos while they're cutting our budgets—who are *they* to preach values to us?" one manager in the plagued realty investment group of the company asked. A former employee of a large bank had this to say about the company's oft-repeated credo of "respect for the individual": "It was seen as a pious lie, given their ruthlessness toward people both within and outside of the organization."

If top-down statements of strategy are prone to encounter cynicism and indifference, statements of corporate values are even more likely to do so. And for similar reasons. They are often seen as disconnected from reality and too general to be acted upon. In addition, such value statements carry with them an emotional content that can be volatile. The teaching of values is generally seen as the responsibility of parents and perhaps schools—something that needs to be done in childhood. Corporate-wide declarations of values may bring such connotations with them.

The key to making formal, written value statements vital and relevant, then, is to connect them with action. Without this connection, they can actually be detrimental, breeding cynicism and resentment.

IN SUMMARY . . .

Creating focus through the formulation of a vision is no easy task. The vision must be crafted with substantial input from leaders at all levels of the organization, it must be based in reality, it must be reflected in action, and it must incorporate the fundamental purpose and key values that drive people in the business. Only then can a vision accomplish its true purpose of guiding and aligning behavior in a way that propels the company toward future success.

BALANCE

In addition to clarifying the organization's strategic focus, successful leaders are adept at balancing what may seem to be competing demands. The balancing act takes several forms:

- Clarifying the strategic focus while at the same time attending to the downsides of that focus
- Being decisive when it is required while encouraging others in the organization to make decisions as well
- Helping the organization change when it needs to while maintaining a sense of consistency and learning from experience

BALANCING THE UPSIDES AND DOWNSIDES OF FOCUS

Strategic focus itself inevitably involves some downsides that must be managed by strategic leaders. Exclusive emphasis on a specific set of goals and strategies may make the organization myopic and inflexible, cutting it off from new opportunities and approaches. Leaders need to pay constant, vigilant attention to balancing the benefits and drawbacks of the selected strategies in order to keep their businesses supple and competitive.

Although alignment of external conditions, goals, and strategies is certainly desirable, there are inherent dilemmas involved with the unilateral pursuit of any strategy. For example, a successful startup business, or what we call an Eagle (see Chapter 9), is usually characterized by people who can live with ambiguity and thrive on innovation and risk. In the real world, however, those qualities have to be balanced with some attention to consistency and standardization. An organization whose formal strategy calls for product innovation, rapid growth, and high risk will still need to codify what it learns by moving toward greater efficiencies, financial controls, and incremental improvements in its existing processes.

Consider the experience of Tandem Computers. In its beginning years, it enjoyed enormous success by exploiting a previously untouched market niche: the need for fault-tolerant computers. Sales increased to $1 billion in its first decade. It grew to 5,000 employees but still had no cost accounting system. When competition entered its market and profit margins became important, managers found that they had no way to collect data on the profitability of individual products. While innovation was still the key to their success, they began to recognize that they also needed routines, efficiencies, and systematic procedures to support their growth.

Large, well-established businesses face the opposite challenge. They must focus on leveraging their strengths by systematizing procedures and creating technological efficiencies in order to take advantage of the considerable experience that has been built up in the organization. Learning from experience means that the business becomes more expert in knowing what needs to be done and how to do it. The challenge in institutionalizing such learning is to do so without becoming closed-minded. People can too soon forget *why* they are doing what they are doing. Leaders of established, successful organizations must balance the competing demands of control and flexibility. Businesses that are known for their ability to achieve such a balance include 3M and Asea Brown Boveri.

Businesses that are pursuing a strategy of rationalization, or slimming down, also face dilemmas that need attention from their top leaders. Rationalizations must be enacted with both speed and deliberation, while maintaining a respect and compassion for the people involved. James Autry describes this leadership balancing act as follows: "The leader must . . . care for people and fire people, sometimes the same people."[17]

An effective slim-down leader needs the ability and courage to "bite the bullet," to streamline and cut back operations, though the cutbacks will be painful. Leaders in this situation have to rely on rational and logical criteria and are less likely to base strategic decisions on the needs and feelings of others. Though such sensitivity may conflict with what has to be done, the feelings of the people who remain will have a significant impact on the success of the strategy. Choosing the right kind of leadership team for such a situation is critical; a leader's style and skills should be supplemented by others who can manage and minimize the emotional repercussions of the slim-down process.

Resolving these contradictions, managing these dichotomies, is one of the most important ways in which strategic leaders help the business stay vital and competitive. The most effective leaders do so by:

- Accepting and managing the evolutionary nature of strategy-making and allowing for deviations from the formal plan
- Allowing different kinds of organizations to be run in the manner best for them; they avoid forcing consistency between business units, except when absolutely necessary
- Staffing the organization with people who have diverse styles and skills

In particular, it can be helpful to think of this strategic balancing act as the responsibility of the top management team, rather than the job of a specific individual. Studies have concluded that the skills and predilections of the full management team, rather than merely the CEO, are the better predictor of organizational outcomes.[18] Instead of asking a single executive to manage all the apparent contradictions involved with running a complex business, make the team responsible for the tightrope act. This requires that the top team be composed of people with diverse skills and preferences.

For example, a new general manager was brought into a company to revitalize a mature business with a broad array of products. Though the business continued to yield high profits, it needed to develop new products and discover new markets in order to be viable in the long term.

The new general manager had been chosen because she was creative and inclined to take risks, to innovate and inspire others in the organization. She recognized, however, that the organization also needed to maintain its solid current businesses. She knew that her strengths did not lie in the area of nurturing those existing efforts, so she chose to concentrate on R&D and marketing, and staffed her top team with leaders who were expert in the core businesses—areas where she was weak. This general manager was smart enough to use her style and strengths in the service of the new focus, while recognizing that leaders with complementary strengths were needed to balance her own limitations.

Having a top team composed of leaders with a variety of styles and strengths is also a recognition that different functions and departments contribute to the strategic direction in a variety of ways. The challenge is to manage each in a way that is consistent with the strategy while recognizing the unique nature of each function. Those functions should act in harmony rather than in unison. Strategic direction is best served by a blending of complementary approaches, not a lockstep alignment.

Such a balanced team has been referred to as a "leadership constellation."[19] In creating such a constellation, the leader of the top team must consider:

- What qualities and strengths would be key complements in this particular business?
- Are there substantial types of managerial skills and leadership styles that are lacking in the current group?
- Can those be developed among existing members, or is it necessary to bring new members with those styles and skills onto the team?
- How can people who see the world in different ways work together effectively and appreciate their differences?

Whatever their individual strengths and weaknesses, the members of the top team need to share some key capabilities for the constellation to be successful. These include the capacity and willingness to grow and change, flexibility to allow strategies to emerge, knowledge of their own strengths and weaknesses, and a tolerance for those with other styles.

BALANCING DECISIVENESS AND PARTICIPATION

The best leaders we know, including Gordon Mounts at Union Carbide and Allyn Keiser at Canadian Imperial Bank of Commerce, are undeniably decisive. You know where they stand, and they are unafraid to take action, even when the data they have are less than conclusive. ("A decision," Arthur Radford comments, "is the action an executive must take when he has information so incomplete that the answer does not suggest itself."[20]) They see themselves as catalysts for change; they take controversial stances that challenge the status quo of their organizations. Yet they also realize that a vision and the strategies needed to achieve it do not spring fully formed into their minds. And they understand that gaining the commitment of the people they work with is of paramount importance.

Wider participation in strategy-making means that senior managers, more than ever, must find a delicate balance between being decisive when required and encouraging others to make their own decisions. How, for example, does a leader help a large, traditionally hierarchical organization make the transition to one that uses the skills of leaders at all levels? "How," one executive wondered, "do we change culture from command-and-control to teams? Can you order people to be participative?"

Interestingly enough, some leaders report doing just that. The 3M executive who instituted one of the first uses of cross-functional teams admitted, "I felt that team leaders ought to be self-selected. But they couldn't self-select because no one really knew what a cross-functional team was, and they didn't volunteer. So we had to bend a few arms to get team leaders in the beginning."

Even when the transition to a team-based organization is successful, there is a balance that has to be maintained. David Kirjassoff, Director of Organizational Performance at National Semiconductor, reports:

> We had a problem of what I'd call "teamamania." Actually, in talking to other companies, this tends to be a common problem. But once you start getting teams going, they tend to naturally form and go at a faster rate than they are actually able to be sponsored and guided. . . . There is a ten-

dency to use teams as a kind of first resort, and not to think through when a team is really necessary. Sometimes what you need is a pretty smart individual to go and figure something out.

One way effective leaders achieve that balance between participation and decisiveness is to clarify the process to be used to make various kinds of decisions. Which kinds of decisions will be made by teams? Which decisions require consensus? On which kinds do the leaders want input but reserve the right to make the final call? At what level of the organization will certain decisions be made? When can they be overruled? In every organization, there is an identifiable process for making decisions; in many, however, the process is not made visible and explicit.

For a leader, knowing when to step in and when to back off requires an intimate in-depth knowledge of the actual work being done in the business. When new senior managers are brought into organizations from outside companies and even from very different industries, they bring new perspectives and often major change. The downside of the practice, however, is that leaders can lack an understanding of what people in the organization actually do and how they do it.

For example, when John Sculley moved from Pepsi to Apple Computer, he brought much-needed marketing expertise to a company that had traditionally been technology-driven. While his marketing savvy did prove to be an asset, his unfamiliarity with the high-tech nature of the business led him to make promises that the technology couldn't fulfill (for example, with the Newton message pad). He also neglected to focus Apple on improving its manufacturing efficiencies and later found that it had to play catch-up with its competitors in terms of its cost position. As Sculley demonstrated, it is often difficult for leaders who are new to their industries to recognize when to intervene in the decision-making process and when not to.

BALANCING CHANGE AND CONSISTENCY

The final aspect of the senior manager's balancing act is to help the organization change direction when required, while at the same time ensuring that it nurtures its key strengths and the positive aspects of its existing culture. Conventional wisdom in what Tom Peters calls the "nanosecond nineties" is that change is occurring more rapidly than ever before and that leaders must transform their organizations into ones that are constantly changing to meet the evolving needs of the market.

Kurt Lewin, a management theorist who devised one of the earliest conceptual models of organizational change, posited a three-step process. At the beginning of the change process, Lewin suggested that the organization is "unfrozen" from its current state. During the transition phase, the change occurs. The organization is then "refrozen" in its new, transformed state.[21]

Today, with change as one of the few "constants" you can count on, few organizations have the luxury of such a discrete process. Instead of transitioning from ice cube to water and back to ice, the best we can hope for is a kind of continual Slurpee. In most businesses today, there is never really a "frozen" state (perhaps there never really was).

Recognition of the continuous nature of change and the chorus of cries for transformational leadership are meant to be a wake-up call for large companies that have grown complacent and lethargic. Certainly many organizations do need to develop the capability to change and to react to changes in their industries more quickly and nimbly. However, focus on transformation alone leads to chaos, unless it is supported by some internal continuity, some recognition of the value of past lessons learned, and some maintenance of the systems that keep the organization operating smoothly.

Therefore, strategic leaders have to know not only what the organization needs to change but what it does *not* need to change. That knowledge comes from a deep understanding of and appreciation for the business's core strengths, in addition to its weaknesses. Acknowledging and building on strengths is often the harder part of the task.

We have conducted strategic planning sessions for approximately 150 organizations over the past ten years. During those sessions, we ask the strategy team to list their organization's strengths and weaknesses. Invariably, the list of weaknesses is considerably longer than the list of strengths.

The healthy side of people's propensity to focus on weaknesses is that it supports continuous improvement. "Everything's coming up roses" may have been a big hit for Ethel Merman, but it is death for a business. But minimizing the importance of your organization's strengths can be equally dangerous. By strengths, we mean the areas in which your business is equal to or better than your competition.

Here are some specific questions to ask in order to identify key strengths:

Customer Position

- Do you have strong brand reputation and image? Are you well thought of by buyers?
- Is your customer base diverse and numerous?
- Do you have special relationships with key customers?
- Are you forward integrated (close to the end-user of your products or services)?
- Does your organization have people with strong marketing and sales skills?

Product Position

- Are you insulated in some way from strong competitive pressures?
- Do you have a distinctive competence in terms of quality, service, or performance?
- Do you supply the full line of products and services in your industry?
- Are you a recognized leader in technology?

Market Share

- Is your business an acknowledged industry leader? Is your market share increasing?
- Do you compete in most or all the markets served by the industry?
- Do you have the ability to raise prices? Will others in the industry follow your lead?

Resource Position

- Does your cost position provide economies of scale and cost advantages?
- Are your facilities state-of-the art?

- Are you back integrated, or do you have ready and consistent access to the raw materials you need?
- Are you able to acquire additional resources and people with the skills you need?
- Do you have special relationships with suppliers?

The strengths identified in this analysis are the keys to maintaining some sense of consistency in the midst of changing circumstances and shifts in strategic direction. Of course, the strengths you choose to leverage and nurture must be matched to opportunities in the industry environment overall. It will do little good to emphasize strengths that customers don't value.

Therefore, it's useful to pair your examination of key strengths with a view of the prospects for the industry overall. Attention to the external factors likely to affect the business in the future has been "rediscovered" lately, most notably by Gary Hamel and C.K. Prahalad in their book *Competing for the Future*. They maintain that organizations have become too focused on their internal strengths and competencies, ignoring the value of external analysis and foresight. While theorists have repeatedly shifted their emphasis from internal to external factors and back again, we maintain that both are important considerations in the strategy process.

Here are some questions you can use to identify external opportunities that will impact your business in the future:

Growth

- Is industry volume increasing? Does growth exceed the growth in the GNP?
- Are your industry's products replacing those in other industries (for example, paper milk cartons replacing glass; home video viewing replacing movie theaters)?
- Are your products safe from being replaced by products from other industries?

Competitive Environment

- Are your competitors few in number and similar to each other?
- Is the distribution of market share in the industry becoming more stable?

- Will tight supply conditions result in increases in the price of your industry's products and services?
- Is there a boom time coming for the industry?
- Do competitors in the industry sell their products on the basis of differentiation rather than price?

Market Environment

- Is there still room for expansion in the product lines offered by the industry overall?
- Do you see possible extensions of the industry's product line into new uses and markets?
- Is there a high rate of technological change?
- Does the industry serve numerous and diverse customers?
- Do industry products provide good value for their price?

External Factors

- Is it difficult for new competitors to enter the industry?
- Will a scarcity of resources drive prices up in the future?
- Will government intervention in your industry lessen?

Such an analysis should be accompanied by a corresponding look at the business's internal weaknesses (where do we have significant deficiencies compared to our competition?) and external threats (what conditions in the external environment could make the industry less attractive or could diminish profitability?). Out of those examinations, leaders decide not only what needs to change but what current efforts and strengths should be safeguarded.

Of course, there are times, based on the information gathered, when the organization really *does* need to make a major shift in strategic direction. That can occur when there is a significant change in the environment or industry, or when the business has not done a good job of adapting to incremental changes in the past. When such a fundamental change is required, the impetus best comes from top management. And those senior managers must recognize the need for such a shift before external conditions create a crisis and it becomes too late for the organization to react effectively.

In spite of our emphasis on the importance of senior management teams, individual leaders, in fact, often do serve as the catalyst for this kind of sweeping change. Strategic leaders at other levels can do an excellent job of adapting strategies and prompting new ones to emerge, but a timely, wholesale change in the vision for the organization can be impelled only by leaders at the top.

One of the key jobs of the strategic leader, then, is to recognize when external or internal conditions affecting the business have changed and to lead the organization in a new direction at the right time. Knowing when the time is right for such a major shift comes from years of experience, finely tuned intuition, careful listening to people both within and outside of the organization, and, to some degree, luck.

Leaders initiate and manage change by:

• *Focusing on the most critical changes.* People in the organization need specific targets for change and improvement—and the fewer targets they have, the more likely it is that these targets will be achieved. Leaders not only inspire people to reach for new goals, they highlight which goals are most critical for strategic success. Robert D. Kennedy, CEO of Union Carbide, did just that from 1986 to 1993. His relentless focus on cutting the chemical giant back to its core businesses and on reducing costs helped Carbide boost its profitability and left it well positioned for the cyclical boom in the industry in 1994.

• *Identifying barriers to change.* Changes are often blocked by the existing systems, processes, and culture of the organization. Anticipating those barriers and finding ways to minimize or overcome them is a key to the implementation of new strategies and new ways of working. Barriers often come in the form of people who resist the new efforts. When CEO George Hatsopoulos placed renewed emphasis on teamwork at Thermo Electron, not everyone was able to make the transition. His advice: "If you find someone who really cannot, no matter how capable he is, *cannot* by nature, develop into having team spirit, you'd better get him out."

• *Communicating clearly and consistently about the changes that are required.* Strategic change requires consistent and persistent communication—two-way communication—about the new vision, and frequent reinforcement of the business's fundamental purpose and critical values. When Jerre Stead headed AT&T's Global Information Solutions, his visible leadership was cited as one of the key elements of the major change in culture. Shortly before Stead left that position, AT&T's Diane Rawlings put it this way: "One of the things he has done very well is to give that vision to the associates. People believe what he says, especially in the international areas. He has established a lot of credibility through his satellite broadcasts and by making himself available through e-mail and 'Ask Jerre' newsletters. People believe that if their own middle management is not going to change, Jerre will do something about it."

Former GM CEO Roger Smith has also emphasized the importance of communicating strategy effectively, and the downsides of not doing so: "I sure wish I'd done a better job of communicating with GM people. . . . Then they would have known why I was tearing the place up, taking out whole divisions, changing our whole production structures. . . . I never got all this across. There we were, charging up the hill right on schedule, and I looked behind me and saw that many people were still at the bottom, trying to decide whether to come along."[22]

Balancing change with consistency, focus with flexibility, and decisiveness with participation—those are some of the key aspects of the strategic leader's tightrope walk. A tough job? You bet. Are there easy answers about how to do it well? There are not. But the best strategic leaders, you can be sure, don't try to do it alone. They marshal the strengths, the knowledge, the skills of people throughout the organization to increase their chances of strategic success.

COORDINATION

Finally, effective leaders of organizations are placing increasing emphasis on coordination among the various units, functions, and businesses in their purviews. Cross-functional coordination is one of the management mantras of the 1990s. It is seen as a way to impel established and traditionally autonomous units out of their insulated silos and to get them to work more closely together in the service of the customer.

The role of strategic leaders involves setting up the systems, processes, and culture that encourage such coordination when it is necessary for the strategic success of the organization. Often, such coordination takes the form of information sharing, allowing key learnings from one part of the organization to be transferred to others. General Electric has done a good job of this kind of coordination through its efforts to disseminate "Best Practices" throughout its many businesses.

Other organizations are experimenting with giving leaders at all levels experience in various businesses and functions. Ray Shaw, a vice president and general manager at NMR, a division of Varian Associates, says: "We intentionally try to move people around. It fosters teamwork. And before you know it, the different functions are talking more to each other."[23]

In addition to setting up systems that encourage cooperation across the organization, senior managers themselves need to share information and often resources with other members of the management group. As such, they form what may be the ultimate cross-functional team. In order to get work done through their peers, senior managers find that they must rely less on the power associated with their positions and more on their personal power and influence (see Chapter 10).

One organization that is focusing on helping top team members coordinate their work more effectively is the Tennessee Valley Authority. In 1994 TVA organized its top forty executives into what it calls the "business council." "The primary goal," the Strategic Planning Manager, Sylvia Caldwell, reports, "is for them to understand every piece of TVA's business, to jointly formulate an overall strategy for where TVA is going, and then for all of them to work toward that strategy. The real goal is for them to be making their daily operating decisions based on this question: 'Does it directly relate to that long-range strategy, and how can we do what's in the best interests of TVA overall?'"

TVA is also in the process of involving a wide array of key people in Strategy Development Teams to conduct a competitive analysis of the energy industry and TVA's position in it. Planning teams will then take that analysis and determine how to springboard TVA into new competitive market opportunities. This broad, cross-business participation in planning is being spearheaded by the business council and the executive committee. It's one of the ways the utility is working on the issue of coordination.

Reengineering, which focuses not on the functions of the business but on the core processes required to serve customers, is the most current "answer" to the coordination challenge. A core business process is a flow of activities that leads to a product or service for an external customer. The idea, then, is to shift our view of the organization from a vertical one with components such as manufacturing, research, and marketing to a horizontal one with processes like customer service and logistics and commercialization of technology (see the illustration).

The main contribution of the reengineering approach is that it encourages an organization to see itself from the customer's point of view and to emphasize those elements that customers actually value. This is

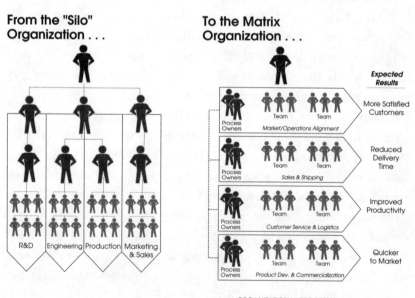

ORGANIZATIONAL PROCESSES

Credits: Adapted from Tony Mikolajczyk for FORTUNE/Source: McKinsey & Co. © 1992 Time Inc. All rights reserved.

not a new concept; management experts from Frederick Taylor to Mary Parker Follett to Len Sayles advocated cross-functional coordination long ago. Until recently, however, large corporations in particular ignored this idea for too long.

Despite the benefits of the reengineering approach, it's important to recognize that it will not *solve* the problem of how to coordinate between functions and units. Core processes themselves, after they have been identified and charted, can become just as fixed and independent as functions once were. Look at that graphic again. The boundaries around the core processes are just as distinct as the lines delineating the functions are. After companies have made the considerable shifts and restructurings that let them focus on core processes, we suspect that they will be asking this question: "How can we get the core processes to work together more effectively in the service of the customer?"

Coordination and cooperation between people who do different things in different places is a problem that will never be solved once and for all. It will be an ongoing challenge and an ongoing role of senior management. The key to meeting this challenge lies in the active day-to-day involvement of management in the business. The degree of coordination required depends on how much the customer needs, either directly or indirectly, the skills of people in various units. Instead of looking at coordination as a blanket corporate mandate, senior executives have to spend time seeing what kind of coordination is required, when, and for what purpose. Only then can coordination really provide the competitive advantage organizations are seeking.

IN SUMMARY . . .

Strategic leaders focus not only on what the organization should emphasize but also what it will *not* do. They often need to protect the organization from a constant barrage of new initiatives, which diffuse energy and make it difficult for people to make decisions in line with the strategic direction. Organizations, especially large ones, can have so many diverse programs and projects under way that any action can be justified because it is connected to at least one of those initiatives. Consider this lament from a senior executive trying his best to transform his organization:

> We clearly have to become more customer-oriented and responsive, okay? But we are in the process of taking out several thousand jobs. And we have processes in place that are going to be extremely difficult to manage with that many people. So, we have a reengineering project as well. In other words, what we are trying to do is improve service, while delivering it with 10 or 15% fewer people, with the necessity of changing the way we do the work. . . . Transitioning our business to a real honest-to-God competitive business is a new thing for us. People don't want to make that change. They seriously don't want to make that change.[24]

Based on this brief statement, we suspect that the problem is not that people in the organization don't want to change, but rather that they are unsure *how* to change, because the strategic focus has not been defined clearly enough. With so many diverse efforts going on, how do individuals really understand what to do differently? The challenge for a senior executive is to create such a clear focus while leaving room for people at all levels to be flexible, creative, and responsive.

PART THREE

Becoming a Strategy Expert

Key Skills for Strategists at All Levels

9

How to Think Like a Strategist

Whosoever desires constant success must change his conduct with the times.
—Niccolo Machiavelli[1]

As we have shown, many companies are redesigning their strategy development processes to incorporate input from leaders at all levels and to recognize that strategies are continually evolving. They are creating strategy-making teams. They are clarifying the new roles and responsibilities of people at all levels in the process. These changes in systems and roles, however, will yield the desired results only if people in the organization have the skills and perspectives they need to think strategically.

An effective strategic thinker, first and foremost, is able to connect his or her daily actions with the longer-term goals of the business. In the traditional sense, that means making decisions that are consistent with the organization's strategies. It also means understanding when the strategies themselves need to evolve in response to changes and potential shifts in the marketplace. In that way, strategic thinking is a close cousin of systems thinking, an approach popularized recently by Peter Senge in *The Fifth Discipline*. At its core, systems thinking involves seeing the interconnected nature of things—how one part of the whole affects and is affected by others.

Strategic thinking is best learned through experience, not in the classroom. However, it can be difficult to synthesize the lessons of experience on the job, because it's often next to impossible to see the results of our actions over time within a complex system. Strategy by its very nature looks to and tries to shape the future. The results of a specific decision are often clouded by time and by many other events that have occurred since. In addition, the hectic pace of most people's daily work leaves little time for contemplating what they have learned.

To help people develop their strategic thinking skills, therefore, it can be useful to augment the lessons of on-the-job experience with more structured activities like training programs and action-learning experiences. Those events provide a chance to examine the results of a decision within a relatively controlled and safe environment, one that allows time for experimentation and contemplation.

While strategic thinking has recently been a key focus in executive development programs and some workshops for middle managers, people at other levels of the organization generally have not been exposed to structured experiences designed to help them learn how to think strategically. As they become more intimately involved with strategy-making, this historical imbalance will need to be corrected.

The essence of strategy is that each organization discovers a fit between its unique capabilities and strengths and the specific opportunities it sees in the marketplace. No two situations are alike. However, in our strategy work with companies over the past fifteen years, we have codified several key principles of strategic thinking that seem to apply in many industries, in many specific situations.

Whatever your level in the organization, these principles can serve as general guidelines to help you think more strategically and fulfill your role as a strategist more effectively. We should stress, however, that these are only guidelines, not *rules*. They are descriptions of what many effective strategists seem to do, not prescriptions to be applied in a blanket way to every organization.

These principles are divided into four general categories, conforming to the kind of business you are in and the thrust of the strategies you are pursuing. We call these categories "strategic states."[2] Which describes your business unit most accurately?

- We are creating a new business, product, market or industry (Eagle state)
- We are an established business; our focus is on maintaining or improving on our current position (Fort state)
- We are slimming down by trimming our product lines, production facilities, distribution systems, or markets served (Slim Down state)
- We are currently in a crisis, and are fighting for the survival of our business (Circled Wagons state)

IF YOU KNOW WHAT STATE YOU'RE IN . . .

As you review those choices, you may recognize your business immediately. Although some efforts and projects currently under way may best be described by a different strategic state, the overall pattern of your strategies and purpose is clearly reflected in a single category. If that is the case, you'll want to focus on the strategic thinking principles related to that state.

IF YOU DON'T . . .

On the other hand, you may have trouble identifying which state best describes your business. Your organization may be pursuing strategies in two, three, or even four of the categories. You are not alone. In our work with executives from a wide array of industries, a diffused strategic focus is one of the most prevalent issues. When we ask people to identify their units' current strategies, they often report a smorgasbord of activities covering two or three strategic states. A business may be rationalizing its old product lines, introducing new ones, and reengineering a key work process. The new products call for great investments of time, attention, and money. As old products are phased out, those managers who were adept at maintaining smooth operations may begin to feel obsolete themselves. The new process flow is less than smooth, and resistance to change is high. How do leaders within a single organization do all these things at once, and do them well?

Successful strategy requires focus, and efforts that fall into multiple strategic states *within the same business unit* can scatter that focus. Such a diversity of strategies can make it difficult for people in the organization to make their own decisions—a key requirement for the new strategists' success.

When people are unsure about which of the competing strategies is most important, they will usually emphasize the strategies with which they feel most comfortable. Within a single business or unit, then, it is critical to identify the primary strategic state or general category of strategies that describes the focus of the business's efforts.

Let us emphasize that we are talking about strategic focus *within a particular business unit*. A business unit has its own defined market, has identifiable competitors in that market, and has at its disposal all the components and resources required to compete in the market as defined. While a large organization will undoubtedly be composed of business units in various strategic states, in our experience, the units themselves are more effective in formulating and implementing strategies if they are focused on one state.

If such a focus is lacking for your business unit, what can you do to clarify it? To some extent, the answer depends on your role in the process. Here are a few preliminary suggestions:

- *For the front-line strategist.* If you are unclear as to which category of strategies is most salient for your business unit, the first step is to ask for clarification. Since it is difficult to pursue very divergent strategies effectively and simultaneously, you are probably already making assumptions as to which should receive the highest priority. It's important to the success of the organization and to your own success that you check those assumptions.

If the answer to your call for clarity is not forthcoming, recognize that the leaders of your unit may be trying to balance competing demands and perhaps even conflicting directives from above. In such a case, you'll need to do the same, to the best of your ability.

And don't overlook the fact that you can *provide clarity* in addition to asking for it from others. Where do you think the organization should be headed? Which approach do you think is the best for your customers? If you still think strategy is none of your business, go back and read the story of Harold Faig of Cincinnati Milacron in Chapter 1. While the leaders at the top of your organization may not always agree with your ideas, as a new strategist, you will take the initiative to propose them.

• *For the strategy integrator.* As the leader in the middle of your organization, you need to clarify the strategic direction for people in the business unit. In addition, you ensure that the systems are in place to help people do their work in a way that is consistent with that direction. For example, if your organization is pioneering a new product, entering a new market, or even aiming to create a new industry (an Eagle), elaborate procedures and extensive company rulebooks can hamper the efforts of innovators. In a more established Fort organization, certain processes do have to be systematized to take advantage of efficiencies that have been developed.

Within a business unit, especially a large one, certain functions may need to be managed differently. An accounting department staffed with risk-taking, unconventional people who are drawn to Eagle strategies would probably be undesirable (in addition to being highly unlikely). However, accountants within an Eagle organization should understand how this business and its strategies differ from those of a more established business.

Effective strategy integrators provide the clear strategic focus people need to make their own decisions in line with the strategy. They are also constantly on the lookout for signs that the strategies are *not* working, and they push for strategic shifts in direction when required.

• *For the strategic leader.* If you are managing a portfolio of different businesses, it is likely that they will be in a variety of strategic states. You may be deemphasizing or slimming down one at the same time as you are building new products and adding staff in another. The important thing is to make sure that the strategic direction is clear within each business unit and that you don't try to run them all the same way. That is one reason why it's so critical to delegate as much decision-making authority as possible to the units themselves: They know what systems, processes, and strategies are most likely to spell success in their specific markets.

If you are unclear about what the strategic state of your unit is or should be, review the suggested strategic planning process, which is outlined in Appendix B of this book. Once you have clarified your general strategic direction, review the principles of strategic thinking related to the strategic state of your business.

PRINCIPLES FOR STRATEGIC THINKING

EAGLE

Eagles are keen-sighted, strong, and fearless; they attack prey that can be overwhelmed swiftly and without warning. Like the eagle, a business in this state is looking for opportunities that previously have gone unnoticed or have been unavailable to others. Eagle strategies are used to manage the creation of a new business, product, or market. The efforts are new to the company, at least, if not new to the world. The snackfood industry was not a new industry, but it was new to Anheuser-Busch when it acquired its line of snacks, appropriately called the Eagle brand. It needed, therefore, to use an approach and strategies different from the ones used to run its existing businesses.

Eagles may also be entirely new companies. In either case, such startup businesses work best when they are run differently from more established ones. Here are some key principles:

Keep the Eagles out of the Fort. Businesses or functions in a startup mode need plenty of autonomy and freedom to find new opportunities. Trying to fly an Eagle using the same kinds of procedures as a Fort is usually a mistake. "Those red-tape antibodies come up and try to snuff you out," one AT&T manager, who was struggling to run a new venture housed within an established business, remarked.

Thermo Electron's "spinout" strategy exemplifies the notion of the separation of different kinds of businesses. In the late 1970s the founder, George Hatsopoulos, felt that the company was not meeting one of its goals—to combine an entrepreneurial culture with the administrative and financial power of a large business. "Our concept was always to do both," Hatsopoulos notes. "In other words, attract entrepreneurs, let them run, but support them, and support them more than a venture capital firm could because we have people who have already gone through the wringer and have found all the difficulties and know what to avoid."

This concept worked well when Thermo Electron was smaller. As it grew, however, entrepreneurs became less and less motivated by such incentives as stock options, because they could less easily connect their own work to the performance of the large enterprise, and because they felt hampered by the whole structure and bureaucracy.

As a result, Hatsopoulos says, "we set out to see if we could have our cake and eat it too." Thermo Electron began spinning out the parts of the company that were working in distinct technological areas. Each division has its own president and publicly traded stock, but all of them also continue to receive administrative support, financing, and advice in business development from the "parent company," which retains majority ownership. "This strategy," one journal reported, "gives Thermo the heft of a 300-pound lineman but the agility of a cornerback."[3]

Don't declare war on a Fort. In most cases, Forts have more resources at their command than less-established Eagle businesses. When an Eagle attacks a Fort, for example, by dropping prices and trying to take market share, the Fort will invariably fight back. With its superior resources, the Fort is likely to win. When Borland, a high-flying Eagle of the software industry, began to compete aggressively against market leaders like Microsoft, Lotus, and Ashton-Tate by undercutting prices, Microsoft beat Borland at its own game by introducing a $99 database program. "You can argue that our pricing strategy came back and bit us," a former Borland director recollected. "Live by the sword, die by the sword."[4]

Borland was not alone in that kind of strategic misstep. When Cott Corporation, a maker of private-label, store-brand sodas, began to eat away at the market shares of Coca-Cola and Pepsi in Canada and Great Britain, the giants dropped prices in those regions by 30 percent and increased incentives to retailers. The counterattacks had a negative effect on Cott's 1994 profit margins and stock prices. "Investors have seen that Coke and Pepsi can make Cott's life difficult," one analyst remarked.[5]

Likewise, Checkers Drive-in Restaurants enjoyed great success in the early 1990s with fast, cheap, and limited menus of burgers and fries. In 1992 it was rated the fastest growing restaurant chain in the United States. Unfortunately, when Burger King got wind of Checkers's success, it fought back with a 99-cent burger and a renewed emphasis on its core menu. In 1994 Checkers moderated its expansion plans and lost money for the first time since it went public. "Somebody woke the elephants," the head of its former advertising agency commented.[6]

Instead of waking the elephants, the most successful Eagles find a unique niche and try to stay out of the giants' paths for as long as possible. Eventually, if a business is successful, it will grow into an established Fort and compete against other Forts. The timing of this shift in strategic states is critical. Cocky Eagle businesses, coming off a string of successes, can easily misjudge the power of their industries' leaders and head directly for strategic disaster.

Get yourself some risk-takers. People who work in businesses in the Eagle state must be prepared to deal with unknowns and to accept high risk. Other important traits include creativity, flexibility, and the ability to handle problems independently.

Too often, people are chosen to lead startup businesses based on a strong track record in more established operations. Unfortunately, their skills and strengths may turn out to be liabilities in their new situation. For example, one large manufacturing conglomerate launched a new electronics component business. The business, based on a new technology that allowed them to make silicon wafers for integrated circuits at about half the cost of the traditional technology, was quite promising. Just as the business was taking off, however, the general manager left and was replaced by a leader who had been quite successful in one of the Fort's established businesses. Using the same approach that had worked for him in his past position, he imposed numerous policies and procedures, and brought in other senior managers with whom he felt comfortable. The business stalled. Later, it was sold for a fraction of what it might have been worth.

This principle does not ignore the fact that people can develop new skills and perspectives over time. Research has shown that providing leaders with new kinds of job challenges is often instrumental to their development. However, this kind of change is enormously difficult for many people, and some may not be able to make the transition. Therefore, it makes sense to staff a new business with a good number of people who prefer to operate in this kind of environment.

FORT

An Eagle establishes its nest in a defensible area and increases the size of that nest year after year. If it has a distinct advantage and is run well and strategically, an Eagle business will eventually become a Fort. A Fort business usually boasts a leadership or strong position in its industry. The word Fort comes from the Sanskrit word meaning "to strengthen or elevate." Companies that follow these strategies do exactly that. They strengthen their existing organizations and may continue to elevate their market position over that of their competitors. Once an Eagle, Microsoft is a big Fort now, as are many of the companies profiled in this book.

We recognize that the fort metaphor is a military one and may seem at odds with our contention that strategy needs to dissociate itself from its military roots. As you might guess, we do not mean to imply that the fort is run by a single general, with foot soldiers carrying out his demands. However, a fort is the best image we can find to describe the principles of strategic thinking related to this kind of business. Those principles include the following:

Clarify the goal: to maintain or to gain? The overarching decision for a Fort, the one that drives the selection of specific strategies, is whether to maintain your current position or to penetrate the market. Maintaining position means growing *with the market* and keeping the *same percentage of market share* that you have now. Market penetration means capturing a *larger share* of the market from your competitors.

Maintaining current position does not mean stagnation. If you are a leader in your industry, or if your industry is enjoying rapid growth, maintaining share is a monumental task in itself. It requires a continuing pursuit of excellence, innovation and improvement of your product line and services, increased differentiation from your competitors, and constant attention to marketing. Remember, as a Fort, you are constantly in danger of being attacked by other strong competitors and by new entrants into your territory.

Market penetration aims to *increase* your current market share. That is usually done by manipulating your marketing mix: lowering price, increasing the value of your products and services, advertising more aggressively. In 1994, when Ford Motor Company's Alex Trotman said, "We are going to be the world's leading auto company," he was essentially announcing a market penetration strategy against GM, Fiat, Volkswagen, Toyota, and Nissan.

Market penetration is the equivalent of declaring war, and the risks are always high. The strategy may be used offensively or in response to an attack by others, when you have no choice but to strike back. Even if your strategy is to maintain position, an attempt by a competitor to take your market share away may draw you into a market war. Market wars pit one Fort against another and will require all your resources until your strategic goals are achieved or the strategy is abandoned.

As the airline industry has demonstrated, market wars can prove detrimental to the industry overall, lowering profit margins for all competitors. While market penetration appears to many to be the most attractive and proactive approach, it's a dangerous strategy, and one that should be considered carefully before embarking on it.

Do it the best. Regardless of whether you are trying to maintain market share or to gain it, you must surpass your competitors in some critical areas in order to succeed. Getting more people in your organization involved in strategy-making is a competitive advantage in this quest. When front-line strategists have the leeway to respond online to customer needs, when strategy integrators can create the goals and approaches that are right for their markets, your organization is building the infrastructure and skills you need to win in the marketplace.

In addition, learning to do it the best requires just that—*learning*. This means, in a nutshell, using experience to help guide the work of the organization in the future. Learning from experience is a key asset of the successful Fort organization. Somewhere in the organization, people have "seen it, done it, been there." And they have lessons to share with the rest of the business.

In the past several years, organizational learning has become a hot topic in the business world. Our definition, based on research conducted by Boston University's Executive Development Roundtable, combines elements of what leaders in the field mean when they speak of organizational learning. Organizational learning occurs when an organization encourages all of its members' ongoing development and uses that learning to achieve and continuously redefine its strategic goals.

A Fort's ability to maintain or grow depends on the ability of people in the business to acquire and use new knowledge and skills—or, very simply, to become continuous learners. Alvin Toffler, in his book *Future Shock,* talked about a survival kit for the future; "knowing how to learn" was one of the highest-priority skills. It was also at the top of the American Society for Training and Development's list of the most important workplace skills in a recent survey of the top corporations in the United States.

Unfortunately, large organizations in particular have not always created that kind of learning environment. Too often they promote routine, procedural responses within a fear-of-failure climate that encourages survival behavior rather than proactive learning.

Leaders at all levels play three key roles in enhancing organizational learning. First, they are learners themselves. "Learning is the very essence of humility, learning from everything and everybody," J. Krishnamurti wrote. "There is no hierarchy in learning." Second, they are also teachers. They become involved in development through mentoring, facilitating seminars, coaching project teams, and so on. At Home Depot, which *Fortune* magazine ranks as one of the most admired corporations in America, founders Bernard Marcus and Arthur Blank continue to lead training sessions, even though the company now has 70,000 employees.[7]

Finally, leaders set up the systems that encourage people to learn: training and development systems, job rotations, feedback systems, and ongoing improvement efforts. The aim of all of those efforts is to ensure that an established Fort organization continues to learn, grow, and evolve.

Replace thyself. Effective Fort organizations do not hesitate to develop new products and services, even when such efforts may threaten existing lines of business. Some have called this practice "eating your lunch before someone else eats it for you." Hewlett-Packard is well known for its willingness to replace its own products. HP's laser printers compete against its own line of cheaper ink-jet printers, and the ink-jet models are steadily taking market share away from the more expensive printers. CEO Lew Platt says: "We have to be willing to cannibalize what we're doing today in order to ensure our leadership in the future. It's counter to human nature, but you have to kill your business while it is still working."[8]

IBM's top executives, on the other hand, were faulted for being unwilling to cannibalize their mainframe computer business, and thus for lagging behind other competitors' innovations. Belatedly, they realized their error, but playing catch-up is tough in the computer industry. Despite impressive profits in 1994, IBM still generates too great a percentage of its revenues from the mainframe business, a worry card for CEO Lou Gerstner and the organization.

In essence, Forts renew themselves by launching new Eagle businesses. The Fort's resources are used to develop the Eagle businesses; the successful Eagles will eventually become Forts in their own right. The strategic challenge is to manage the two kinds of business separately and to find ways, despite this separation, to coordinate their efforts when it is beneficial.

SLIM DOWN

Not every business achieves the ideal cycle of the Eagle becoming a Fort, the Fort spinning off Eagles. Without constant attention to continuous improvement, a Fort can easily become fat. Past decisions that determined appropriate product lines, market segments, and organizational structure may not continue to benefit the current business if the environment has changed. The growth of the existing organization may have slowed or stopped, but the Fort systems, structure, and staffing often survive.

A business in a Slim Down state needs to diet. This analogy is appropriate in several ways: With good habits, careful monitoring, and frequent adjustments, dieting would never be necessary. Barring major shifts in the industry environment, an organization that has made a habit of adjusting to its environment should not have to go into a Slim Down state. However, if any of those factors slip (and they apparently often do), the key is to recognize the need to slim down, to do it as healthily as possible, and to move on (with the hope of retaining those better habits).

The need for Slim Down strategies can also be triggered by fast-changing conditions in an industry, conditions that no longer allow for adequate returns. The need to slim down as a result of cyclical conditions varies widely from industry to industry. In the 1970s, the entire chemical industry found itself in a Slim Down state. Oil companies and resource-rich countries moved into chemical production, leaving existing producers with overbuilt capacity. They undertook major rationalizations of plants and products. In the mid 1980s the pendulum began to swing the other way; capacity could not keep up with demand, and the chemical Forts enjoyed a tremendous boom. The late 1980s and early 1990s saw another major shift. The cycle continues.

A company pursuing Slim Down strategies might choose to rationalize its product line, production, distribution, or markets. In an extreme case, it may pare back to its "little jewel" or most profitable piece.

Here are some key principles to follow should you find yourself in a Slim Down state:

Do it fast; get it done. Whatever the cause, a quick response to conditions indicating the need for a Slim Down is critical. Those companies that respond to new threats by slimming down swiftly and compassionately often emerge as the healthiest and most vigorous competitors in their industries. In many companies, however, ground is conceded grudgingly and at considerable expense. When Slim Down strategies are not identified early and made a conscious, common goal, the Slim Down state can become debilitating. That is a lesson Pan Am learned the hard way.

Just as a diet can be taken to extremes, the health of a business can be compromised if the Slim Down is taken too far for too long. Long-term use of this set of strategies can lead to crippling concessions to competitors and irreversible damage to the organization. In a 1994 study by the American Management Association, two-thirds of the corporations that reported slimming down their headcount one year followed up with the same process the next year. "These repeat restructurers," *Fortune* reported, "rather than becoming lean and mean, often end up lean and lame."[9]

The tendency to prolong a Slim Down by executing it in slow motion is natural and human. Leaders often want to avoid the task, recognizing that it will be painful to people in the organization. However, in their desire to spare the business pain, they can actually cause even more harm by drawing out the process.

In the pilot phase of a new research project, the Center for Creative Leadership found that "respondents whose organizations had experienced significant employee reductions within the last two years, when compared to respondents whose organizations had not experienced downsizing, [were] less secure in their jobs (67% versus 88%), less confident in their leaders (75% versus 85%), less likely to believe what their leaders told them (76% versus 87%), less likely to trust their leaders (75% versus 87%), and less hopeful about the future of the organization (86% versus 93%)."[10] It seems logical that people in organizations that are engaged in a prolonged Slim Down feel even less hope and even more skepticism.

The emotional repercussions of a Slim Down cannot be avoided entirely. However, they can be minimized by slimming down quickly; they can also be exacerbated by doing so slowly over a number of years.

You can't involve people enough. As with the implementation of any strategy, involvement of people at all levels is a key to success. The Slim Down strategies, however, present certain obvious dilemmas that are not associated with other strategic states. Decisions about whom to keep and whom to lay off must be made by management. There are, however, a wide range of other decisions that are best made by others throughout the organization who have the most intimate knowledge of the workings of the business and the greatest sense of where inefficiencies are lurking.

Bob Thrasher, an executive vice president at NYNEX, sought the input of just such experts when he took the helm of that company's downsizing effort. He organized eighty NYNEX people into four teams and gave them the task of reducing operating expenses 35–40 percent. They dispatched themselves throughout the business, and came up with more than three hundred recommendations for specific Slim Down changes.[11]

As leaders invite more people to participate in the Slim Down process, there is a great deal to be said for candor. Using such terms as "reengineering" and "restructuring" to cloak a downsizing effort can create a trust gap that inhibits true participation. Pitney Bowes Management Services conducted a 1994 survey with some sobering results: Of the largest industrial corporations they surveyed, 83 percent said that they had reengineered their businesses. They also said that their employees:

- See reengineering as an excuse for layoffs (69 percent)
- Fear the loss of their own jobs (75 percent)
- Feel overburdened by work (55 percent)[12]

Jerry Miller, an ex-employee of US West, described the nightmare of working himself out of a job: "When we first formed our teams, the company came in talking teamwork and empowerment and promised we wouldn't lose any jobs. It turns out all this was a big cover. The company had us all set up for reengineering. We showed them how to streamline the work, and now 9,000 people are gone. It was cut-your-own-throat. It makes you feel used."[13]

With such understandable and extreme emotions at work, leaders of downsizing organizations owe it to the people in the business to be as honest and forthcoming as is humanly possible. If you are a leader of your organization, you may not be able to save everyone's job, but you can at least be candid about the purpose behind your efforts in order to preserve their dignity and self-respect.

If you are a strategist on the front lines of your organization, your task is equally difficult. You may essentially be asked to put yourself or your colleagues out of a job. If this is the case, you have two choices. You can either resist the Slim Down efforts in the hopes that your job will be one of the ones that is saved, or you can get on board. Those are certainly not enviable options, but if your organization is in this condition, they are the only ones you have. If you do decide to help in the downsizing efforts by offering your expertise and knowledge of where cuts could be made most effectively, you at least have the possibility of proving your strategic worth to the organization and thus increasing your chance of remaining a part of it.

Attend to the survivors. Perhaps the most insidious result of a Slim Down effort that involves layoffs is that the morale of those who remain can be deeply affected. This is a key reason for enacting a Slim Down quickly. Even if the change is done swiftly and compassionately, however, the people who remain in the organization can experience a great feeling of loss, and that feeling can affect the organization's ability to move forward.

Robert Axtell, director of DuPont's worldwide nylon business, reminds us: "You can't communicate enough, because there is a lot of confusion when you restructure." Spend time to "do healing" with the people who remain. "You must spend a lot of time teambuilding with the people who are left."[14]

Perhaps one of the most effective ways of enlisting the commitment of those who have survived a downsizing is to get them more and more involved in the strategy-making process. That will provide them with a deeper understanding of the need for the relatively drastic measures that have been taken and a clearer view of the conditions that precipitated the changes. It can also help them regain a sense of control and belonging that is often weakened by the layoff process.

CIRCLED WAGONS

A business in the Circled Wagons state is faced with extremely difficult times or a crisis that requires a major restriction of operations and an immediate suspension of whatever other strategies are being pursued. In the life of a business, there may be events that are so life-threatening that they require the suspension of all current strategies until the environment stabilizes. Like pioneers who positioned their wagons in a circle to protect themselves, the business establishes a short-term goal of surviving a potentially deadly attack; it enters the Circled Wagons state.

Business strategies consistent with this state may be as simple as delaying current plans or investments, or as severe as divesting segments of the business to placate attackers or to provide revenue to stave off a takeover threat. Short-term crises are often handled by edict management, which may involve cutting budgets across the board or placing restraints on new investments. Other survival techniques include financially restructuring the company, eliminating management positions or replacing leaders in the management chain, and freezing capital investment. High-level executives, including the chairman, may be called on to "save the company" by making personal appearances or sales calls to preserve key accounts.

Union Carbide after the Bhopal disaster and the GAF takeover attempt found itself in a Circled Wagons state. All efforts went toward survival. UCC went into debt and divested its battery, antifreeze, and other consumer products businesses. During that period, the Eagle and even the Fort businesses were at a standstill. They held on until after the crisis passed.

Johnson & Johnson after the Tylenol contamination, and Audi with its reported sudden acceleration problems, were also in the Circled Wagons state. So, arguably, was Intel with its much-publicized Pentium chip debacle late in 1994. Although Intel reported strong earnings despite the controversy, the division's glitch in its chips threatened its credibility and undermined its relationships with alliance partners and customers.

Here are some key strategic principles, should you find yourself in this undesirable strategic state:

Take the bull by the horns. This is obviously not a state that you want your business to be in. If you are there already, however, you don't want to stay there very long. Therefore, it is imperative to recognize the threat, to take steps to deal with it, and to move on.

Ignoring the crisis will not help. When IBM first came forward with its claims about the unreliability of Intel's Pentium chip, Intel's CEO Andy Grove stated that "the reaction is unwarranted." When public and press pressure intensified, Intel instituted a policy of replacing the chips only for people who could prove that they used them for complex mathematical calculations. When that approach proved a disaster, Grove said: "To some people, this policy seemed arrogant and uncaring and we apologize for that." The public relations nightmare was halted only when Intel agreed to replace the chip for anyone who requested it.

Although it can be argued that Intel averted a Circled Wagons crisis of life-threatening proportions, it did so by the skin of its teeth. Circled Wagons conditions, especially in consumer businesses, are often brought on by press and consumer concerns, and a strictly rational approach to problems of this sort will not suffice. If your customers *think* you have a problem, despite what you believe, you *do* have a problem. The more people you have in direct contact with those customers, and the more you can get their input and impressions, the better the chance that you will perceive the problem the way your customers do. And that puts you several steps ahead in dealing with it.

Rally. Despite the more participatory approach we advocate in most of this book, the Circled Wagons approach requires a certain degree of command-and-control leadership. The keys to responding to such a crisis are speed and a broad perspective. Although wide involvement in strategy-making can increase the organization's ability to make quick decisions in an ongoing way, there are times when a major decision has to be made very rapidly in response to a cataclysmic event. In such a case, only the top leaders of the organization have both the power and the broad perspective to make the decision quickly.

Top leadership also must communicate to the rest of the people in the organization, clearly and forcefully, about the absolute need for the solutions that have been decided upon, the rationale behind them, and the vision for the future of the business after it emerges from the Circled Wagons state.

Don't cry wolf. If your business is facing a situation that threatens its survival in the short term, dealing with the crisis promptly is imperative. However, too many businesses live for too long in a perpetual state of agitation and anxiety because of a protracted Circled Wagons mentality. That occurs most often when a Slim Down has been dragged out and people feel, despite evidence to the contrary, that the existence of the enterprise is in danger. That creates an extreme version of the fear-of-failure mentality and blocks the people in the organization from responding in a flexible way to cues from the environment.

The Circled Wagons mentality can be inadvertently promoted by leaders who are trying to catalyze major change in their organizations. Instead of inspiring commitment, however, those rallying cries often engender fear and skepticism. They can also make the organization less ready to deal with *real* crises when they do occur.

The other important reason why, in our experience, some leaders cling to the Circled Wagons state long beyond its usefulness is that they enjoy being generals. As we have noted, crisis demands strong and at times autocratic leadership. People in the business will accept that kind of direction much more easily during a crisis than they will at other times. For a leader who thrives on power, who prefers to make decisions alone, the Circled Wagons state can seem strangely fulfilling. Especially if he or she has led the company through the crisis, the temptation to keep on commanding and controlling can be very seductive.

IN SUMMARY . . .

The principles outlined above for each strategic state are only a few. Strategic leaders at all levels will and should, of course, develop their own guidelines to help them navigate the straits and narrows of strategy. That is the essence of strategic thinking. The trick, when you boil it down to the essentials, is knowing when to generalize from experience and when to invent a new set of guidelines. It's the same challenge that faces us all in our daily lives: knowing when to apply the knowledge we have to new situations and when a new approach is required. As with any dilemma, the answer probably lies somewhere between the two extremes.

No matter how strong your strategic thinking skills are, you will need the help and support of others to determine the best strategic approach and to implement it flexibly. Strategy-making comprises two interlocking components: thought and action. In this chapter, we've emphasized the former; the next chapter focuses on action—how to get other people's commitment to strategic initiatives that will contribute to your business's success.

10

Getting It Done

How to Gain Support for Your Strategic Initiatives

There comes a time when you have to stop revving up the car and shove it in gear.
—David Mahoney[1]

However sound your strategic thinking skills, however brilliant your plans, they amount to nothing unless you can get them implemented. Leaders at all levels must avoid the temptation to think that planning itself—even planning done with a great deal of participation by others—is sufficient for strategic success. While few would say, as Phillipe August Villiers did, that "I have thought too much to stoop to action,"[2] too many strategy-makers still behave that way. The traditional separation between those who plan and those who do, between formulating strategies and implementing them, may have encouraged leaders to pay insufficient attention to translating plans into action.

DEGREES OF SUPPORT

Implementing strategy virtually always requires the support of others in the organization. You cannot do it alone. Support from others can be seen as a continuum, with extraordinary commitment on one end and fierce resistance on the other. In the middle of the continuum, you'll find compliance. While in the real world you may have to settle for compliance from time to time, your effectiveness as a strategist depends on your ability to get commitment from the key people who need to be involved in order for the strategies to succeed.

COMMITMENT

Commitment brings with it self-discipline that does not need extensive monitoring. People who are fully committed put in discretionary effort. (Think of discretionary effort as the maximum amount of effort possible minus the amount that is absolutely necessary to keep your job.) They not only do what they've agreed to do, they discover better ways to accomplish the work. They take on the objectives as their own. They may even come up with more ambitious goals and strategies.

In a team-based organization commitment takes on added importance, because the work of the team members is so interdependent. Lack of commitment by one team member can affect the ability of the entire team to do its job well. Dan Wilkowsky of National Semiconductor put it this way:

> You can't do all of the teamwork in a team meeting. The key lies in the commitment of the individuals to do the work once they leave the conference room. And sometimes that's tough because when they get back to their desks, they've got a whole lot of work, and their traditional bosses are giving them all kinds of assignments. But when someone commits to the team to have that portion of the effort done, they wouldn't dare come back to the meeting with it undone, unless there was an earthquake or something. I know how bad I feel on my softball team if I leave a couple of batters on base at the end of the inning. It's the same thing—nobody is going to hold up the work of the rest of the team members if they can possibly help it.

Even when the work of the people within the team is done with commitment and conviction, the team usually has to enlist the support of others in the organization in order to get their strategies and recommendations implemented. David Kirjassoff, also with National Semiconductor, noted that "what we found when we did research on our cross-functional teams was that it was generally not too hard for someone to learn how to be an effective team member. But a lot of the problems they had were, 'How do we get direction and sponsorship?' and then, 'How do we influence the organization to make the changes that we are coming up with?'"

COMPLIANCE

Peter M. Senge says, "Real commitment is rare in today's organizations. It is our experience that 90 percent of the time what passes for commitment is compliance."[3] Compliance occurs when a person does exactly what you ask him or her to do (but no more) in support of your strategic initiatives. Of course, there are some cases where compliance is all that is required (for example, completing a very simple, routine task or following a safety policy). However, compliance is unlikely to result in innovative, collaborative solutions to a problem and is likely to require more monitoring and oversight than true commitment does. In terms of strategy, a person who is compliant rather than committed to the goals is less likely to identify evolving strategies or to raise the red flag when new information is uncovered.

RESISTANCE

At the opposite end of the continuum from commitment is resistance. Resistance means that the person is opposed to your request or plan and tries to avoid carrying it out. Such resistance may be obvious or subtle. The person may seek to have the request nullified by upper management or may delay acting in the hope that you are not serious about it. Perhaps most damaging is hidden resistance, where the person pretends to comply but tries to sabotage the effort.

Your role as a new strategist means that you need to find ways to turn resistance into compliance and to turn compliance into commitment. That is part of an ongoing process of amassing the support you need to translate strategy into action.

Your ability to gain other people's support is based on two factors: your power and your influence. Let us explain in more detail what we mean by each.

POWER

In essence, power paves the way, making it easier for you to influence others and to gain their commitment. People often associate power with position on the organizational chart. The closer you are to the top of the chart, the more power you have. While that may indeed be true in many cases, it's only one part of the picture.

Our colleague, Toni Lucia, likes to tell the story of Bob, who worked in the tool room of a large manufacturing facility. Bob was responsible for signing out the tools used by all the people on the plant floor each day. Although he did not even appear on the organizational chart for his business, Bob wielded a lot of power. If he liked you, a new, operative tool was always available. If he didn't, you would find that the tools you needed had either already been signed out or were broken. While Bob did not always use his clout for the betterment of his organization, he did have power.

There are essentially two types of power: position power and personal power. *Position power* is your potential to influence others based on your position in the organization. While that kind of power may indeed be related to your place in the hierarchy, the notion of position power is changing. Position power can be divided into four categories:

• *Authority or legitimate power:* Your right to make requests of others, within the scope of your job responsibilities and role in the organization. While a boss obviously has authority to make requests of the people who report to her, everyone has this type of power to some extent. You have a right, for example, to ask your boss for a performance review. As a member of a cross-functional team, you have the right to enjoy access to information you need to create strategies and make decisions.

• *Reward power:* Your control over tangible and intangible things other people want. While the ability to control tangible rewards like pay increases or bonuses is often related to your position in the hierarchy, people throughout the organization can provide intangible kinds of rewards such as help and support (or, in Bob's case, functioning tools).

• *Power over negative consequences:* Your control over punishments or the denial of expected rewards. The power to create negative consequences is most often thought of as a top-down dynamic. However, people often have this kind of power over their bosses. For example, they can refuse to take on assignments, can do work more slowly than usual, or can even threaten to quit. (Obviously, the use of this kind of power can ultimately be detrimental.)

• *Information power:* Your access to information other people need and may not be able to get from other sources. Front-line strategists, with their more direct pipeline to customers and markets, may actually have as much information power as the CEO.

Position power alone, however, is usually not enough to ensure commitment. While people may comply with your requests because you are the boss or because you have control over rewards, they are unlikely to put in extraordinary effort for those reasons. Leaders who are most effective at gaining commitment from others, therefore, build on their *personal power* rather than their position power. "The ability to problem solve is power," Colombe Nicholas notes. "The ability to interact—to effect conciliation, compromise, team spirit. . . . that is power. . . . You don't have to conform to some stereotype of a tough-minded executive in order to have and use power. In the final analysis you have to be yourself."[4]

Personal power comes from two principal sources:

• *Expertise:* Your credibility as a source of advice, based on your knowledge and experience
• *Admiration or identification:* People's esteem for you and their belief that you have exceptional qualities

Personal power, which is becoming a much more important trait in today's less hierarchical organizations, is not fixed. It changes over time. When you enter a new organization, for example, your personal power may be quite low, because you have not yet developed relationships or had a chance to demonstrate your expertise. Over time, however, you can build that power by suggesting courses of action that meet with success. You can also build personal power by developing deeper and broader expertise—by keeping informed of advances in your field and by sharing your knowledge with others.

"Leadership is not just about where you are positioned in the organiza-tion," Dr. Kenni Crane, Director of Management and Organizational De-velopment for CIGNA, observes. "It's much more about your personal influence and whatever skills and strengths you have to bring to accom-plishing the difficult work of the organization." CIGNA's Property and Ca-sualty Division offers associates the opportunity to get feedback on their personal power and influence through the use of a 360-degree question-naire. (A 360-degree questionnaire provides feedback from all "direc-tions"—bosses, colleagues, and people who report to you.) CIGNA also offers training programs aimed at helping people develop and refine their influence skills. Many other organizations, including General Electric, The New England, Allen-Bradley, and Boeing, are doing the same.

A final note about power. It can, for some people, carry with it con-notations of absolute control over others, of manipulation. We all know that power can be abused; it can also be used constructively to help a business achieve its strategic goals. As long as you are using your power to help your business rather than for your own aggrandizement, to con-vince rather than command, power can be instrumental in achieving your initiatives and helping you fulfill the demands of your new strate-gic role.

THE NEW STRATEGIC SKILL: INFLUENCE

Even extensive position and personal power, however, do not guarantee that people will be committed to helping you develop and implement strategies. You must actually *exert* this power by trying to influence peo-ple. While that may seem a somewhat obvious statement, it's a key learning for many. People are often surprised that their colleagues be-lieve they seldom try to influence them. As a strategy-maker, your effec-tiveness depends on your willingness to take initiative, to take a stand, and to persuade others to join you in your quest.

Think about the people you know who are the best at gaining your commitment. What, specifically, do those people do? How do they do it? Because influence skills are becoming more and more critical in organizations today, we have conducted ten years of research into the topic. Essentially, we set out to discover:

- What approaches people use to influence each other on the job
- Which approaches are most likely to result in commitment, compliance, and resistance
- Which approaches are used most frequently by people who are seen as very effective

The remainder of this chapter will describe what we found out from questionnaires completed by more than 2,500 people in a wide array of organizations and industries. Most of them work in U.S.-based corporations; the highest percentage were middle- and senior-level managers, although individual contributors and people at other levels were also represented. The development of the survey and much of the data analyses were conducted by Dr. Gary Yukl and his colleagues at the State University of New York at Albany.

CORE INFLUENCE TACTICS

The people who are seen as most effective in gaining the commitment of others use three basic approaches, or what we call "core influence tactics":

- *Reasoning:* Using logical arguments and factual evidence to persuade people that your strategy, proposal, or request is viable and likely to help the business achieve its goals
- *Inspiring:* Presenting a strategy, proposal, or request in a way that arouses enthusiasm and appeals to people's values and ideals.
- *Consulting:* Seeking people's participation in planning a strategy, activity, or change, and being willing to modify a proposal to deal with their concerns and suggestions

Of course, any tactic, including those cited above, can result in resistance if it is not used skillfully, or if it is not appropriate for the specific situation. Whether or not an attempt to influence is successful depends on a variety of things: the approach used, the relative power of the people involved, their past relationship, the skill of the "influencer," and the attitudes and perceptions of the person being influenced. However, across a broad array of situations, reasoning, inspiring, and consulting were most effective in gaining the commitment of others.

Although for research purposes it is useful to describe and study the various influence tactics separately, in real life they are usually used simultaneously or in a series. People often blend the tactics together, or use one as a follow-up if their first or second try has not given the results they want.

Reasoning. Reasoning is by far the most extensively used of all the influence tactics. People use this approach in over two-thirds of their attempts to influence others. Reasoning, the research indicates, is the best predictor of effectiveness ratings given by the boss of the person involved. In other words, people who used reasoning more frequently were more likely to be rated high in effectiveness by their bosses.

Examples of reasoning, which has also been called rational persuasion, include explaining the reasons for your request, explaining how the other person would benefit if he or she supported you, and providing evidence to show that your plan or proposal is likely to succeed. For example, if you are proposing that your business embark on a new strategy, you could refer to a report containing positive results from a pilot study or to a market survey showing that customers would respond well to a new product or innovation. You could also provide documentation about expected costs and benefits or explain how the approach was used successfully in the past.

Another aspect of effective reasoning is anticipating people's concerns and dealing with them directly. Review some possible problems with your proposal and show how they might be overcome. Show how you propose to avoid problems, overcome obstacles, and minimize risks.

Reasoning is used more frequently when people are trying to convince those who are in a higher position on the organizational chart than when they are dealing with their colleagues on the same level or with people who report to them. That may be because people are used to the idea that they have to convince their bosses, but feel that simply telling their subordinates what to do is sufficient. It will be interesting to see if the ongoing research detects shifts in the use of reasoning as organizations rely less on the hierarchy and more on delegation and on cross-functional teams.

Reasoning is a familiar tactic for many managers, especially in the United States. It is the foundation of our business school programs and implicit in the selection process as people rise to higher levels in their organizations. Assessing cause and effect and making logical arguments supported by facts are core skills in the world of business.

Even though reasoning is, in general, one of the most effective ways to influence people, it cannot be relied on as the only way to do so. While logic may be compelling for many people, others are influenced more by appeals to their emotions and values. In addition, true commitment, rather than mere compliance, engages the heart as well as the mind. Reasoning, then, is often combined with other approaches by the most influential leaders.

Inspiring. While reasoning appeals to the head, inspiring appeals to the heart. Inspiring aims to develop enthusiasm and commitment by linking your proposals to people's values, hopes, and ideals. Values that can be particularly inspiring include the desire to accomplish something worthwhile, to do something exceptional, or to participate in an exciting effort to make things better.

We tend to think of inspirational people as larger than life: world leaders, popes, renowned humanitarians. However, think of the people in your life who have inspired you. The list probably includes some who were not famous but who changed your life in an important way. Inspiring, then, is not just the work of those who give speeches, or those at the top of the organization. It is a powerful influence tool that can be used effectively by people at all levels.

While inspiring is one of the three core tactics that builds commitment, it is the most difficult one for many to learn to use. "I'm just not rah-rah that way," people will remark. "I'll look stupid." It's important to realize, however, that inspiring need not be done with great fanfare. It can be just as effective in a quiet one-on-one conversation. For example, if you know that your colleague values the recognition of other experts in her field, and you are asking her to join a new product development team, you might emphasize that there will be opportunities to publish the team's work in a professional journal. If you know that your boss cares a great deal about environmental issues, and you are asking for his support for a new product idea, you might stress that the new product will be environmentally friendly.

Those examples illustrate one of the keys to inspiring effectively: You must understand what people's values are in order to appeal to them. Assuming that everyone's values are similar is a common mistake. Appealing to a person's desire for achievement when he is really more concerned with balancing work and family time is not likely to get you what you want.

So, how do you find out what people's values are? One obvious way is to ask them. "What's most important to you about your job?" "What do you like best about it?" "What do you like least?" Another way is to pay attention to their behavior—what gets them excited? How do they spend their discretionary time? The more you know about the values of the people you work with, the easier it will be to link their needs and hopes to the work to be done.

Which brings us to another key point about influence: Effective influence is built on strong relationships with specific people. Its foundation is trust, which takes time and a series of interactions to develop and grow. We all know at least one person who comes around only when he needs something. Over time, the relationship erodes, as does his ability to influence you. Influencing isn't just something you do to others—it's a two-way street.

Finally, effective influence is not a sneaky, manipulative ploy to trick other people into doing what you want. The best influencers are overt about their desire to gain your support. They will admit that they are trying to convince you and truly believe that you will both be well served by the approach they advocate.

Consulting. Both reasoning and inspiring are often combined successfully with another core tactic, consulting. Consulting can take many forms, including:

- Asking people to help plan efforts or activities that will require their support and commitment
- Telling people that your proposal is tentative and asking for their suggestions
- Encouraging people to express any concerns or doubts they may have about your plan
- Modifying your proposal to deal with concerns and to incorporate suggestions

The approach to strategy-making described in this book is built on a foundation of consulting. Effective consulting comes from a genuine desire for people's input; it should never be used insincerely. The input must be valued and used, or your ability to influence people will diminish over time.

One key to helping people become more comfortable with giving you input is the way you react to their ideas and suggestions. Especially in an environment that has traditionally discouraged open disagreement, it may take time to build people's trust to the point where they feel comfortable with giving input. Such was the case with the Tennessee Valley Authority, according to one senior manager. In 1992, Craven Crowell took over as chairman, with a very different management style from his predecessor's. "Our former chairman had the tendency to fire people if they did not agree with his opinion, so people were very, very tentative with coming forward with the truth. They have watched what the current chairman has done when they have been honest with him, and they have found that he responds to it very well—he enjoys honesty and appreciates it. As they get more comfortable with that fact, they are being more open and honest with him."

A very basic but powerful technique for reacting to and encouraging input has been around for years. It's called the itemized response. After someone offers an idea or suggestion, first tell them what you liked about it. *Then*, if you have any concerns about it, you can discuss them.

The itemized response does several things. It lets people know that their input is valued, it works to maintain their self-respect, and it preserves the valuable parts of the idea so that you can build on them. It is a very simple technique and has been taught in training seminars for decades. However, as you go through your day, notice how few people use it.

We've all had the unfortunate experience of being asked for our input and then having that input summarily rejected, refuted, or simply ignored. Consulting, when it is done clumsily, may be worse than not asking for input in the first place.

When it is done well, however, it proves to be *the* most effective and useful approach to gaining commitment. Consulting can be effective in all directions—with people above, below, or at the same level on the organization chart. It requires little in the way of established relationships. In other words, it is a good approach to use when you are dealing with people you don't know very well. In terms of strategy, it is the most useful approach for generating strategic options and for discovering evolving strategies.

SUPPORT TACTICS

There are several other approaches to influence that can be effective in certain situations or when used in conjunction with the core tactics cited. We call them "support tactics." Overall, the research indicates that they are less effective than the core tactics, perhaps because they are harder to use well or because they can have more severe downsides. More often than not, support tactics used on their own will lead to compliance rather than true commitment. Support tactics include:

- *Recognizing:* Complimenting people and being friendly and polite to encourage their cooperation
- *Personal Appeal:* Appealing to people's feelings of loyalty and friendship to gain their support and assistance
- *Exchanging:* Making an explicit or implicit promise that people will be given rewards or a share of the benefits if they comply with your request or support your proposal
- *Coalition Building:* Seeking the aid of others to persuade a person to do something, or using the support of others as an argument for why he/she should agree

Recognizing. Recognition can be a powerful motivator and can, over time, increase your ability to influence people. Examples of recognizing include complimenting the person on past accomplishments, saying that he is the most qualified for a task, and expressing understanding and concern for any inconvenience involved with your request.

Recognition tends to be underused by many people, perhaps because they associate it with "brown-nosing." However, when it is done sincerely, recognizing can contribute to more positive relationships, can help people feel better about their work, and can build your own personal power.

Sincerity is obviously the key here. If you say to a co-worker "Gee, I love your tie, now will you do this report for me," recognition won't get you very far. But taking the time to acknowledge a job well done or to compliment a person on new skills she is developing can build a foundation of trust and respect that is important for effective influence.

Personal Appeal. Many people occasionally make requests that are based on their friendship with others. Such requests are usually prefaced by a statement like "I'm really in a jam here. Could you do me a favor and help me out?"

If the relationship is indeed friendly, most people are willing to comply with an occasional personal appeal. This approach becomes problematic, though, when such appeals become too frequent or when what the person is asking is not commensurate with the closeness of the relationship.

Some people use the tactic without really recognizing that they are doing so. If you begin all requests with "Do me a favor?" you may consider this to be a figure of speech. Others, however, may not interpret it that way.

Exchanging. Exchanging is the "You scratch my back, I'll scratch yours later" tactic. Essentially, you offer either an explicit or an implicit promise that the person will get something in return for helping you out.

Exchanging may bring with it the connotation of a bribe, and some people shy away from using it for that reason. In actuality, exchange is often the currency on which many organizations operate. When a colleague offers to do some of your work if you can help her out on a project, that is an exchange. When you cover for someone who is on vacation, and he does the same for you, that is an exchange. Your boss is also using exchange when she extends the deadline on one of your projects so that you can focus on a more urgent matter that she would like you to tackle.

The key to effective use of exchange is in the follow-through. When you tell someone "I owe you a lunch" but never buy it, your ability to influence him in the future may be compromised.

Coalition Building. This tactic involves getting the support of a third party. Examples of coalition building include mentioning the names of credible people who support your plan or proposal, bringing someone with more expertise along with you to a meeting, and asking other people to speak out in favor of your proposal.

Used effectively, coalitions can be powerful methods of getting things done, especially if you have little power on your own. However, they can also result in real resistance if they are used covertly. People can easily feel ganged up on and manipulated by this approach. Therefore, it should be used only in an overt way: "Would it be okay with you if I invited Susan to our meeting? She's a real expert in this area, and I think she has some compelling arguments that you should hear."

LAST RESORT TACTICS

Finally, there are two tactics that should be used only as a last resort. Even when used well, these approaches will result in compliance rather than commitment. They are best used sparingly, because they often damage relationships and will decrease your personal power over time. In some situations, however, they may be necessary.

- *Establishing Authority:* Establishing the legitimacy of a request by showing that you have the authority or the right to make it or by verifying that it is consistent with organizational policies, rules, practices, or procedures.
- *Pressuring:* Using threats, demands, intimidation, or persistent reminders to persuade someone to do what you want.

Establishing Authority. It's important to use this approach only if your authority has been questioned. Leading off a conversation with this tactic shuts the door on the possibility of gaining commitment. Even when a request is legitimate, most people simply do not get enthused about work because they are *supposed* to do it.

How you establish your authority is the key to getting compliance rather than resistance. Consider the following dialogue between a training director and a line manager:

> *Training director:* I need a copy of the performance evaluations for each of your people by December 15.
>
> *Line manager:* Do I have to send them to you? I thought those were confidential.
>
> *Training director:* Look, as Director of Training, I'm supposed to have access to that information.

Now look at a more effective way of establishing authority in the same situation:

> *Training director:* I need a copy of the performance evaluations for each of your people by December 15.
>
> *Line manager:* Do I have to send them to you? I thought those were confidential.
>
> *Training director:* Well, this year, as Director of Training, I've been asked by Don to review all of the performance evaluations. I'm responsible for identifying group strengths and training needs so that we can decide how to allocate our training dollars for next year. You can check with him if you have any concerns.

Especially if you are in a new role, you may at times need to establish your authority. People may legitimately wonder why you are asking them to do something. If they do ask, let them know as specifically and clearly as you can about your new responsibilities.

Pressuring. The final influence tactic is one that is familiar to many people: pressuring. At its extreme, pressure could be a threat to fire someone or to go to his or her boss. However, pressure often rears its head in more subtle ways, such as insistent, nagging reminders, constant monitoring, and sending a copy of a memo to someone's boss.

There are times, of course, when pressure is required, but it should be used sparingly and only as a last resort. Pressure can heighten people's resistance and make compliance less, rather than more, likely. It almost always eats away at your personal power and your ability to gain support in the future.

When pressure is necessary, it's important to describe the problem and the consequences of noncompliance very specifically. General threats like "there's going to be trouble around here" are likely to be perceived as empty. And then, follow through with what you said you were going to do.

DEVELOPING AN INFLUENCE PLAN

As a strategist, being prepared for a key conversation in which you will try to influence someone is fundamental for success. Whether you assess the situation and develop a game plan beforehand or are responding as you go during a discussion, there are some basic guidelines and questions that will help you understand the situation and decide on a plan of action.

- Be clear about the purpose of your influence attempt—what results you want and how you will know when you have achieved them. Your purpose should be focused and specific and should describe what you want the person to do as a result.
- Analyze the situation and the players as thoroughly as you can. Determine which approaches are most likely to be successful, given your analysis.
- Identify an appropriate combination of tactics to help you get off to a good start and get the results you want.
- Let the conversation evolve; don't stick too strictly to a planned script. However, always keep your purpose firmly in mind.

The following worksheet can help you think through the approach you would like to use in a specific situation.

Influence Plan

1. Person to be influenced: _____

2. Purpose of influence attempt (specific change in attitude, perception, behavior):

3. What are this person's objectives, values, and needs?

4. Which core tactics will you use?
   Reasoning
   Inspiring
   Consulting

5. Which support tactics, if any, will you use?
   Recognizing
   Personal Appeal
   Exchanging
   Coalition Building

6. Which of the above tactics will you begin with?

7. What will your opening statement be?

8. What are some possible objections?

9. What is your fallback position if you meet with resistance?

IN SUMMARY . . .

Using your power and influence to gain support for strategic initiatives is a key to being part of the strategy-making process. The most effective strategists use a combination of approaches to gain support, varying their tactics to suit the specific situation in front of them. Overall, though, they rely most on reasoning, inspiring, and consulting. Those are approaches that can be used effectively by anyone, at any level in the organization. (For a brief questionnaire you can use to get feedback on your influence skills, see Appendix A.)

Developing a cadre of people throughout a business who are effective at gaining each other's support is critical to the implementation of any strategy. These skills are also useful in other areas—when dealing with suppliers, with customers, even with family members. Used well, influence builds strong relationships between people in every business and across every function. Through those relationships and conversations over time, new ideas and strategies emerge and are formalized. For this reason, influence skills, combined with the ability to think strategically, are *the* critical tools for leaders at all levels.

IN CONCLUSION . . .

The organizations that are implementing the new strategy-making processes outlined in this book are doing so in three ways: creating the structures and cultures that encourage wider participation, defining the roles of leaders at all levels in the process, and helping their "new strategists" develop the skills they need to make a significant and real contribution to the success of their businesses.

Underlying this shift in strategy-making is a single core value: the appreciation of diversity. A business that values diversity welcomes the input of people with different backgrounds, cultures, experiences, needs, and strengths. Their input is used not to fulfill a government mandate or to placate a specific group of workers but to help the business achieve its full potential and fulfill its fundamental purpose: to make a significant contribution to society in its areas of expertise.

As companies and countries become more closely linked with a variety cultures and areas of the globe, the need for a broader perspective becomes more and more critical strategically. A broader perspective cannot be developed solely by teaching CEOs and other top managers how to think globally and strategically. As companies work to broaden their view of the world and the markets they will serve in the future, they are recognizing the benefits of tapping the diversity in their own backyards: the insights, experiences, predilections, and recommendations of their own associates. By involving leaders at all levels in the art of collaborative strategy-making, they are opening up new windows that allow them to explore more and more possibilities, and those possibilities will form the blueprint for their future success.

We applaud the innovative efforts of the people and companies who have the courage and the foresight to leverage the diversity within them. We have been inspired by your example, and we look forward to your continued success.

APPENDIX A

Self-Assessment Questionnaires

SELF-ASSESSMENT QUESTIONNAIRE
FOR THE FRONT-LINE STRATEGIST

The first step in learning to fulfill this new role as a front-line strategist is to take stock of the current state of affairs. How well are front-line strategists in your organization fulfilling their new roles? If you are in this situation, how well are you doing? We encourage you to take a few minutes to evaluate your own performance as a front-line strategist. Even if you are a senior manager, and therefore far removed from the front lines of your organization, these are qualities and behaviors that you should be modeling for others in your business. Whatever your job in the organization, therefore, it can be useful to think through your own behavior and skills as a front-line strategist. (For more information on the role of the front-line strategist, see Chapter 6.)

For the items listed below, consider how consistently and extensively you fulfill the role of the front-line strategist, using the following choices:

- 4—Usually, to a great extent
- 3—Sometimes, to a moderate extent
- 2—Seldom, to a small extent
- 1—Never, not at all

THE FRONT-LINE STRATEGIST QUESTIONNAIRE

Voice of the Customer

_____ 1. I meet with clients and customers to discover how better to satisfy their needs.

_____ 2. When a customer has a problem, I make sure that it comes to the attention of others in my organization.

_____ 3. I take personal responsibility for making sure that customers are satisfied.

_____ 4. When a company policy or procedure is making it difficult for me to keep customers satisfied, I work to change it.

_____ 5. I actively seek out opportunities to communicate with the leaders of my organization about customer needs and suggestions.

Hunter/Gatherer

_____ 6. I maintain contacts with people outside my organization who can provide information about important developments and events.

_____ 7. I actively search for information about what our competitors are doing.

_____ 8. I keep abreast of new developments and innovations in my area of expertise.

_____ 9. I pass on relevant memos, reports, and other written materials to people who otherwise might not receive them.

_____ 10. I make sure that important information about our markets and customers is seen by others in the organization.

Cross-functional Magnet

_____ 11. I form alliances with people in other units of the organization to work toward shared goals.

_____ 12. I try to understand the point of view of my colleagues in other functions when we have a disagreement.

_____ 13. When making decisions, I consider the good of the business as a whole, rather than only the needs of my specific area.

_____ 14. I maintain contacts with people in other parts of the organization who can be a useful source of information, resources, and support.

_____ 15. I provide help, support, and resources to people in other units when they ask for them.

Some items in this questionnaire have been adapted from *Compass: The Managerial Practices Survey,* a 360-degree feedback instrument developed by Dr. Gary Yukl and Manus.

When you have completed all of the items, add up your total and divide by 15. A score between 3 and 4 indicates that you feel you behave like a front-line strategist much of the time. A score below 3 suggests that you may not be taking full advantage of opportunities to contribute to your organization's strategy-making process.

While rating your own performance is a good start, it can be very helpful to ask other people to give you feedback on these items as well. On questionnaires of this kind, people often rate themselves higher than others do—that is, they intend to do these things, and think that they are doing them more often than other people see them doing so. Ask five people you work with frequently to give you their feedback on the items in this questionnaire. You may be surprised at their responses.

Using the feedback you have gathered, identify several specific behaviors that you would like to be using more often. Ask a colleague or boss to help you monitor your use of those behaviors, and check with that person again in two weeks to see if he or she has noticed a difference. You may also want to read books on the subject of effective information gathering and team membership, attend relevant training courses, or even identify job rotations that will force you to develop these critical skills. (For more information about how to develop your abilities in the areas you've identified, see Appendix C.)

SELF-ASSESSMENT QUESTIONNAIRE
FOR THE STRATEGY INTEGRATOR

Strategy integrators, as we discuss in Chapter 7, have a demanding and critical set of roles to play in the strategy process; they act as ambassadors, facilitators, and jugglers. How well are the strategy integrators in your organization fulfilling these functions? If you are in this role, how are you doing? The brief questionnaire that follows is designed to help you assess your own performance as a strategy integrator.

For the items listed below, consider how consistently and extensively you fulfill the role of the strategy integrator, using the following choices:

- 4—Usually, to a great extent
- 3—Sometimes, to a moderate extent
- 2—Seldom, to a small extent
- 1—Never, not at all

Ambassador

_____ 1. When presenting formal strategies and making recommendations to corporate leadership, I consider both the perspective of my unit and the good of the organization overall.

_____ 2. I explain to people in my unit the reasoning behind the strategic direction we are pursuing.

_____ 3. I appeal to people's values, ideals, and aspirations when describing our strategic direction.

_____ 4. I provide appropriate rewards for people who contribute to our strategic success.

_____ 5. I give public recognition to people who are instrumental to the success of our strategies.

Facilitator

_____ 6. I ensure that my unit develops long-range plans describing the objectives and strategies to be pursued in the coming years.

_____ 7. I ensure that people in our unit understand the process we use to make strategic decisions.

_____ 8. I ask people for feedback about the process we use to make decisions.

_____ 9. I involve people at all levels of my organization in making major changes and decisions.

_____ 10. I identify new strategies that are emerging and, when appropriate, incorporate them into our deliberate strategic plans.

Juggler

_____ 11. I ensure that our unit is staffed with a balanced group of people whose strengths lie in both leadership and management.

_____ 12. I attend to both the long-term and the short-term needs of my unit.

_____ 13. I ensure that we have systems to monitor the work of our unit in terms of both efficiency and effectiveness.

Some items in this questionnaire have been adapted from *Compass: The Managerial Practices Survey*, a 360-degree feedback instrument developed by Dr. Gary Yukl and Manus.

When you have completed all of the items, add up your total and divide by 13. This will give you a score for how frequently you feel you use behaviors that support your role as a strategy integrator.

A score between 3 and 4 indicates that you feel you are behaving consistently with this role most of the time. A score below 3 suggests that you may not be taking full advantage of opportunities to contribute to your organization's strategy-making process.

As with the previous questionnaire, it can be useful to ask others in your organization to give you their feedback after you do your own self-assessment. Remember, people often rate themselves higher than others do on this kind of questionnaire. Self-knowledge depends not only on introspection but also on honest feedback from others.

Using the feedback you have gathered, identify several specific behaviors that you would like to be using more often. Ask a colleague or boss to help you monitor your use of these behaviors. Other development strategies include reading, attending training courses, and taking on job or task force assignments that will help you develop new skills. (See Appendix C on strategies for change to help you identify which approach will be most beneficial.)

SELF-ASSESSMENT QUESTIONNAIRE
FOR THE STRATEGIC LEADER

Strategic leaders, like tightrope walkers, have a difficult and risky job. How well are you focusing, balancing, and coordinating the activities of your organization?

The brief questionnaire that follows is designed to help you assess your own performance as a strategic leader (see Chapter 8).

For the items listed below, consider how consistently and extensively you fulfill the role of the strategic leader, using the following choices:

- 4—Usually, to a great extent
- 3—Sometimes, to a moderate extent
- 2—Seldom, to a small extent
- 1—Never, not at all

Focus

_____ 1. I lead the process of developing a clear and appealing vision of what our organization will be in the future.

_____ 2. I ensure that our vision incorporates the input and suggestions of people throughout our organization.

_____ 3. I ensure that our vision is both challenging and realistic.

_____ 4. I help people in our organization connect our vision to the actions they need to take, by establishing specific goals linked to the vision.

_____ 5. I ensure that our vision reflects people's values, ideals, and aspirations, and describes the fundamental purpose of the business.

Balance

_____ 6. I encourage businesses and functions in the organization to be managed differently, in the manner that is most appropriate for them.

_____ 7. I ensure that our organization is staffed with people who have diverse styles, skills, and strengths.

_____ 8. I ensure that the top management team of the organization is balanced in terms of the styles, skills, and strengths of its members.

_____ 9. I clarify the process by which decisions are made in the organization.

_____ 10. I ensure that our strategies build on the organization's strengths.

Coordination

_____ 11. I ensure that our systems, processes, and culture promote cross-functional and cross-business cooperation when it is beneficial to our strategic success.

_____ 12. I evaluate what kind of cross-functional and cross-business cooperation is required and for what purpose.

_____ 13. I cooperate and share information and resources with other top leaders in the organization.

Some items in this questionnaire have been adapted from *Compass: The Managerial Practices Survey*, a 360-degree feedback instrument developed by Dr. Gary Yukl and Manus.

When you have completed all of the items, add up your total and divide by 13. This will give you an overall score for how often you feel you use behaviors that support your role as a strategic leader.

As with the previous questionnaires, a score between 3 and 4 indicates that you feel you are behaving consistently with this role most of the time. A score below 3 suggests that you may not be leading your organization's strategy-making process with as much focus, balance, and coordination as it may need.

In addition to doing your own self-assessment, consider asking others in your organization to give you their feedback on your performance. People's perceptions, however much you may agree or disagree with them, have a substantial impact on their willingness to follow your lead.

Using the feedback you have gathered, identify several specific behaviors that you would like to be using more often. Begin by asking trusted members of your management team to help you monitor your use of those behaviors. Other development strategies include reading, attending executive development courses, and taking on job or task force assignments that will help you develop new skills. (See Appendix C for strategies to help you identify which approach will be most beneficial.)

INFLUENCE QUESTIONNAIRE

In Chapter 10 we discussed the critical skill of influencing and its importance for you as a strategist.

It is sometimes difficult to assess your own use of influence, because your intent, or what you are trying to do, may be different from your impact on others, It can be useful, then, to enlist the help of people you work with. They will be able to provide you with a clearer picture of your current behavior, which serves as the basis for deciding how you might be more effective. To help you gather feedback from your colleagues, your bosses, and those who report to you, we've included a brief questionnaire. (You have our permission to make copies of it.) Distribute the questionnaire to between eight and ten people with whom you work.

Ask them to complete the survey and to return it to you. If you don't feel that it will inhibit their willingness to give you honest feedback, ask them to write their names on the questionnaire. This can make it easier for you to follow up and ask for clarification on any items you don't understand. However, you should realize that people are often less honest when they know that *you* will know how they responded. If you think this might be an issue, ask them to reply anonymously.

INFLUENCE TACTICS: RECOMMENDATIONS

To the respondent: The person who has given you this questionnaire would like your feedback on how he or she might influence you more effectively in order to gain your commitment to his or her plans, proposals, or ideas. Please give your recommendations on how much the person should use the following approaches when dealing with you. Read the definition of each tactic and indicate whether the person should:

- Use this tactic *more* (write "M" in the space next to the tactic)
- Use this tactic the *same amount* (write "S" in the space next to the tactic)
- Use this tactic *less* (write "L" in the space next to the tactic)

_____ *Reasoning:* using logical arguments and factual evidence to persuade you that his or her strategy, proposal, or request is viable and likely to help the business achieve its goals

_____ *Inspiring:* presenting a strategy, proposal, or request in a way that arouses enthusiasm and appeals to your values and ideals

_____ *Consulting:* seeking your participation in planning a strategy, activity, or change, and being willing to modify a proposal to deal with your concerns and suggestions

_____ *Recognizing:* complimenting you and being friendly and polite to encourage your cooperation

_____ *Personal Appeal:* appealing to your feelings of loyalty and friendship to gain your support and assistance

_____ *Exchanging:* making an explicit or implicit promise that you will be given rewards or a share of the benefits if you comply with the request or support the proposal

_____ *Coalition Building:* seeking the aid of others to persuade you to do something, or using the support of others as an argument for why you should agree

_____ *Establishing Authority:* establishing the legitimacy of a request by showing that he/she has the authority or the right to make it, or by verifying that it is consistent with organizational policies, rules, practices, or procedures

_____ *Pressuring:* using threats, demands, intimidation, or persistent reminders to persuade you to do what he/she wants

When you have completed this questionnaire, please return it to the person who asked for your feedback.

This questionnaire is adapted from *Matrix*, a 360-degree feedback instrument developed by Gary Yukl and Manus.

INTERPRETING YOUR FEEDBACK

When you have received all of your completed questionnaires, tally up the recommendations for each tactic. The chart on the next page can help you summarize your results.

	Number of people who said do		
Tactic	*More*	*Same*	*Less*
Reasoning			
Inspiring			
Consulting			
Recognizing			
Personal Appeal			
Exchanging			
Coalition Building			
Establishing Authority			
Pressuring			

After you have tallied all your questionnaires, see if you can spot any clear consensus on any of the tactics. Do more than 50 percent of the respondents want you to consult with them more? To pressure them less? If so, these are clear areas that you need to attend to and find out more about.

Also look for patterns that might be confusing. Do some people want you to reason with them more, while others want you to do so less?

What explanations might you have for the discrepancy? Do you try to influence your boss one way and your colleagues in other ways? What about your direct reports (those people who report to you)? These are areas that may need more investigation.

SHARING AND CLARIFYING FEEDBACK

After you have reviewed your feedback, it's important to share what you have discovered with the people who responded and to get clear about any unresolved questions. This was, after all, a very brief questionnaire, and you are likely to have questions about exactly what the feedback meant. Arrange to meet with each person separately or with the group as a whole, if that is feasible. Here are some suggested action steps to follow during the meeting:

- *Express appreciation.* Thank the person for providing you with feedback and describe how the feedback was useful.
- *Give an overview.* Provide a summary of your strengths and areas for development.
- *Ask for input.* Ask for the person's input on the areas you have identified, and then offer your ideas.
- *Discuss issues for clarification.* Ask the person to help you understand feedback you found surprising or confusing.
- *Summarize next steps.* Commit to actions you will take based on the feedback and ask for help if appropriate.
- *Ask for ongoing feedback.* Invite the person to let you know how you are doing and set a follow-up date.

If holding such a meeting makes you slightly nervous, you are not alone. Most of us want to know how we are perceived by others; the process can also be uncomfortable. If you are truly committed to improving your own effectiveness and that of your business, however, getting honest feedback is a critical step.

After you have identified areas of strength and areas in which you would like to improve, refer to Appendix C. It contains suggestions for how you might approach the process of developing new skills.

APPENDIX B

Strategic Planning Process

As we have pointed out, the development of a strategic plan often falls to the management team of a business or function. However, it can also be done by teams comprising individuals from all levels. Certain aspects of plan development can also be extremely useful exercises for other teams charged with, for example, product development, process improvement, and marketing.

The formulation of a strategic plan is the process of arriving at a clear consensus of where you are, where you want to be, and how you will get from here to there. Although the strategic planning process will eventually lead to the development of a written plan, this document is not the end goal. The real goal and benefit of strategic planning is a common understanding of your business—now and in the future.

The process outlined in this appendix is designed to help members of a strategy team develop a common understanding of and consensus about:

- your industry's potential for profitability and growth
- the factors that determine competitive success in that industry, now and in the future
- your current and future strategic direction and goals
- the mission and vision statements that describe that strategic direction

199

- how day-to-day activities will be guided by that direction
- how various businesses or functions will support each other and contribute to your overall strategic goals

ABOUT THIS PROCESS

The process described here focuses on the development of deliberate strategy. However, it is important to remember that strategies are also continually evolving in response to changes in the environment, and that those emergent strategies are vital to the strategic process. Evolutionary strategies can be signs of environmental changes, which should prompt a revisiting of the current plan. Be on the lookout for evolving strategies that can be incorporated into the deliberate plan, and be prepared to review and revise the plan often.

This appendix is, by necessity, written in a linear way; strategy itself is never as cut-and-dried. Each business in each industry faces unique challenges and opportunities. True strategy requires flexible and creative thinking. The process steps outlined here are meant to be used as a guide, not a formula.

Throughout this section, we'll emphasize the role of the strategy team in developing and implementing the strategy for the business. This is not to suggest that the members of the team are working in isolation, handing down dictates to the rest of the organization. Throughout the process, members of the strategy team are seeking input from others in their organizations—soliciting their opinions, involving them in the data gathering, and, especially in the implementation phase, providing them with opportunities to contribute directly to the effort to achieve the strategies and realize the Vision. For more detail about how to involve people at all levels in the formal planning process, see Chapter 4.

CLARIFYING THE PLANNING LEVEL

As you begin the planning process, it's critical to recognize the level of the organization that you are planning for. Formal planning can and should be done at three levels:

• Portfolio-level strategic planning involves setting a clear direction for the corporation and integrating the strategies of individual businesses so that they work in synergy with each other and contribute to that overall direction.

• Business-level strategic planning defines the business's role in its industry. Planning at this level identifies the strategic direction of the business unit and integrates the strategies of the individual functions within the business.

• Functional-level strategic planning can be used to focus the efforts of particular functions, product lines, or even segments of product lines within a business unit. However, no function exists in isolation, and relationships between segments must be considered.

INDUSTRY AND BUSINESS DEFINITIONS

Begin the strategic planning process by creating definitions of your industry and business, ensuring a common understanding of who you are and what you do.

These definitions are a critical step in the process, because they establish the parameters for the analyses that follow. Definitions can help you identify the "real" competition and are the first step toward undertaking strategies appropriate for industry conditions and competitive capabilities.

The way you define your business and industry will shape the possibilities you are able to recognize. For example, the DeVilbiss Company began at the turn of the century as a maker of perfume atomizers. Had it continued to define its business as such, it would probably be out of business now. However, it was able to broaden its definition of its product to encompass several uses of the basic spray technology. DeVilbiss now produces equipment used in automobile factories to paint cars, as well as components for compressors and respirators.

Industry and Business Definitions are not "givens." They can and must be defined by the people in the business. This idea has important implications for a misapplied notion that has found its way into strategic planning wisdom: the product/market-segment life cycle, which suggests that a particular product in a particular market goes through predictable stages of growth, maturation, and eventually obsolescence. Some have expanded this valid and useful concept to imply that a business or industry goes through parallel phases in conjunction with its product.

In fact, managing strategically involves recognizing changes in the industry or business over time and redefining the industry so that it continually transcends the life cycles of individual products. The buggy whip industry may be dead, but the vehicle accessory industry is certainly alive. The way strategic leaders define the industry and business is, in fact, the foundation of the strategic process.

Revisit the definitions throughout the strategic planning process to be sure that they accurately reflect your industry and business—each step in the process speaks to the ones before and after.

INDUSTRY DEFINITION

The Industry Definition should encompass all of the required functions, from the creation to the sale of the products/services supplied by companies that compete in the industry. The definition also includes current sales in dollars and/or volume and current market share of key participants.

The Industry Definition includes these elements:

- *Products.* What do we provide to our customers? (e.g., beverages, polyethylene resins, property/casualty insurance, telecommunications equipment)
- *Services.* What services do we provide? (e.g., financial advice, information, consulting) What degree of technical and special assistance is required by our customers? (e.g., customization, blending, training)
- *Customers.* Who buys our products/services? (e.g., container manufacturers, beer distributors, end-users)
- *Markets.* In what ways are our products used? (e.g., farming, construction, personal use)
- *Functions.* What is our role in providing those products/services? (e.g., manufacture, distribution, marketing/sales)

Products/Services: _____

_____

Customers/Markets: _____

_____

Functions: _____

_____

Location/Scope: _____

_____

Industry Size: $ _____   Volume: _____

Competitors: _____

_____

_____

_____

_____

_____

_____

_____

_____

- *Location/Scope.* In what parts of the world do we compete? (e.g., North America, California, worldwide)
- *Current industry and business size* in dollars and/or volume of product sold
- *Major competitors* in the industry

BUSINESS DEFINITION

The next step is to create a Business Definition, outlining the aspects of the industry in which your business participates.

The Business Definition may be fully congruent with the Industry Definition or may include less than the Industry Definition. It should not involve more products/services, functions or customers/markets than the Industry Definition. The definition also includes current sales in dollars and/or volume and current market share of key participants.

Go back to the elements covered in the Industry Definition, and answer each question as it relates to your specific business.

Products/Services:

_____

_____

_____

Customers/Markets:

_____

_____

_____

Functions:

_____

_____

_____

Location/Scope:

_____

_____

_____

Market Share:

_____

Business Size: $ _____   Volume: _____

Key Competitors:

_____

_____

_____

_____

_____

INDUSTRY ATTRACTIVENESS ANALYSIS

After the strategy team has established the parameters for the industry and the business, you will evaluate the external opportunities and threats inherent in the industry environment. In other words, this assessment summarizes your industry's potential for profitability and growth over a specific time period.

The Industry Attractiveness Analysis includes such factors as expected growth, the potential of other products to replace your industry's products, and the possibilities for products of this industry to be used in new ways.

Useful time frames for planning vary from industry to industry. Planning for the rock music industry, for example, would be useful only within a very short horizon. Aircraft manufacturers, on the other hand, would have to plan for a much longer period. Select a time frame that is typically appropriate to your industry's planning needs (e.g., 1–2 years, five years).

Industry prospects vary over time. In this analysis, you will rate industry prospects as *Excellent, Good, Fair,* or *Poor.*

After evaluating each of the variables, review them and sort out the critical few (usually three or four) that will be most important during the time frame. Those are the key factors that will determine industry attractiveness over the time frame you have chosen. Remember, in this analysis you are rating the industry overall, not your specific business.

On the following page, you'll find a chart you can use to summarize your analysis. After the chart, we've provided a description of each of the factors involved. Because the rating on many factors is counter-intuitive (for example, under Product/Service breadth, a narrow product line indicates opportunities to expand and would therefore be rated *Excellent* or *Good*), we recommend that you review the definition of each factor before rating it.

TIME FRAME:	Industry Attractiveness Analysis				
	EXCELLENT	GOOD	FAIR	POOR	√
GROWTH EVALUATION					
Volume Growth					
Replacement Potential					
Vulnerability to Substitution					
Resource Availability					
COMPETITIVE ENVIRONMENT					
Competitive Mix & Number					
Share Stability					
Barriers to Entry					
Cyclicality					
Basis of Competition					
MARKET ENVIRONMENT					
Value Added					
Product Line Breadth					
Breadth & Diversity of Markets					
Technology/Innovation					
Customer Mix & Number					
Government Intervention					
OVERALL					

√ = **Key Factor affecting
Industry Attractiveness**

Volume Growth: First rate your industry's current growth, using these guidelines:

- *Excellent*—Growth rates well above GNP, usually double-digit
- *Good*—Growth above GNP (or GDP), usually 2–3 percent better
- *Fair*—Growth at the same rate as GNP
- *Poor*—Growth below GNP or negative in real terms

Then predict the change in the growth rate of the industry's products. Compared with current growth rates, is future growth likely to be significantly higher or lower? Combine your assessment of current conditions and expected changes to determine an overall growth rating for the planning period.

High-growth-rate industries tend to be less predictable than low-growth-rate industries. In general, the more stable the predicted growth, the more reliable the planning.

Replacement Potential. Evaluate the ability or potential of your industry's products to replace products in other industries (e.g., paper containers replacing plastic, home perms replacing salon treatments). An *Excellent* rating reflects great possibilities for replacing others' products. A *Poor* rating indicates little likelihood that your industry's products will be used as substitutes for products in other industries.

Vulnerability to Substitution. Are users currently substituting your industry's products with those of other industries (e.g., home video viewing replacing movie theatres)? An industry that is relatively invulnerable to substitution would be rated *Excellent* or *Good*.

Over the time frame of this analysis, do you predict any change in the vulnerability of your industry's products to substitution by products outside the industry?

Resource Availability. First, rate the industry now in terms of resource availability. Note: The ratings in this factor tend to contradict apparent logic. Scarcity of required resources is generally beneficial to profitability. When raw materials, skilled personnel, unique distribution capabilities, or other resources are scarce, the value of the industry's products/services often rises dramatically, resulting in an *Excellent* or *Good* rating. The oil crisis of the 1970s and early 1980s is a classic example. When resources are plentiful and available to all producers, there is little chance of differentiation or securing advantages; the rating would therefore be lower (*Fair* or *Poor*).

Competitive Mix and Number. The fewer and more homogeneous the competitors in the industry are, the better the conditions for profitability will be. The more diverse and numerous the competition, the less likely the industry is to be profitable. An *Excellent* rating applies to an industry composed of very few competitors with similar characteristics; a *Poor* rating describes an industry with many diverse competitors.

How would you describe the current spectrum of competitors in the industry? Is this profile likely to change? Are competitors entering or exiting the industry, or reshaping their profiles significantly?

Share Stability. Assess the industry's trend toward stability or instability of share. Is the current distribution of market share likely to shift?

Ironically, in many industries current share stability does not always bode well for the trend of the future. The more stable current conditions are, the more unstable they are likely to be in the future. Unstable current share distribution indicates the potential for stability and better profitability but may require a "shakeout" period. Movement toward stability earns an *Excellent* or *Good* rating; toward instability should be rated *Fair* or *Poor.*

Barriers to Entry. The higher the barriers to the entry of new competitors, the better the prospects for profitability. Barriers are created by proprietary know-how, unique skills, patents, existing franchises, high risks, enormously high investment, and so on. Is the industry likely to become more or less accessible to new participants?

Cyclicality. Assess the industry's tendency to create its own lowered use of investment through the overbuilding of its resources or its sensitivity to economic cycles. Industries subject to economic cycles may face extreme conditions as "boom-and-bust" cycles occur. An industry that is vulnerable to such ups and downs would rate *Fair* to *Poor,* depending on the degree of vulnerability and the severity of predicted economic cycles. An industry that rarely puts itself through such cycles would be rated *Good* to *Excellent.*

Cyclicality is often due to the industry's inability to shift use of its resources in response to demand. For example, the chemical industry makes such mammoth investments in its plants and equipment that those resources must be kept in use fairly consistently regardless of changes in demand. That creates cyclical conditions, because competitors drop and raise prices dramatically in order to keep the volume at a fairly consistent level.

How will the industry react to expected changes in utilization? If tight supply conditions will result in big increases in the price of products/services, the industry is rated *Excellent*. If capacity is expected to exceed demand, and the industry historically reacts to such developments by dropping price significantly, a *Poor* rating would apply.

Basis of Competition. Evaluate the basis for selling the industry's products and services. The greater the ability to differentiate products/services, the higher the likelihood of industry profitability. Without confirmed potential for new and differentiated products/services, the current condition will deteriorate as each competitor learns how to replicate the others' best products and services.

Value Added. Evaluate the value-added structure of the industry's products/services. If the customer perceives the product's value to be high relative to its cost, chances for profitability are better. For example, if you are a fan of a particular recording artist, the cost of the CD or tape is far outweighed by the amount of enjoyment you'll get.

Product Line Breadth. Consider the breadth of the current line of the industry's products/services, and evaluate the opportunities for growth through product line expansion. Extensive product lines are costly to maintain and indicate less opportunity for expansion and differentiation. *Excellent* and *Good* ratings indicate a narrow line with opportunities to expand, while a *Fair* or *Poor* rating reflects an industry that has already fully developed its current products/services.

Breadth and Diversity of Markets. An industry that serves few markets but has the potential to expand into others is generally in a better position than one that has already expanded into many markets. Assess the possibility of expansion into new and different uses or markets.

Technology Innovation. Evaluate the rate of change in the technology and innovation of the industry. For the industry overall, the higher the rate of change, the better the prospects for growth and profitability.

Customer Mix and Number. In general, the larger and more diverse the customer base of an industry, the better the conditions are likely to be. Industries dependent on only a few major customers would be rated *Poor* in this factor. As you rate this factor, try to anticipate changes in the spectrum of current industry customers. Consider changes in the customer base as a result of customer consolidation, expansion into new areas, and the like.

Government Intervention. Evaluate the degree to which government intervention is expected to have an effect on your industry. The greater the chance of interference, the less sure you can be about all the other areas covered by this analysis. Government actions at municipal, state, or federal levels hinder natural market forces and introduce an element of unpredictability. Even actions that seem to be beneficial to the industry are suspect—changes in government leadership can quickly reverse such initiatives.

Key Ratings. During any period of time, there will be three or four variables in the Industry Attractiveness Analysis that will be most critical to the industry's performance. Key ratings are chosen based on the interaction among current conditions, the likelihood of change, the potential impact (positive, negative, or neutral), and the magnitude of the change.

Using the key factors you have identified, agree on an overall rating over the time frame you have selected. Are the prospects for your industry *Excellent, Good, Fair,* or *Poor* over the time frame you have selected?

COMPETITIVE POSITION ANALYSIS

The strategy team has now arrived at an overall rating for the prospects for growth and profitability in the industry. You have also identified the key factors that you feel will determine industry attractiveness over the time frame of the evaluation.

Now you will examine your business in detail and will evaluate your strengths and weaknesses relative to competitors. You will examine your market position, market participation, and ability to take the lead in raising prices. You'll look at your product position, product line differentiation and breadth, and the state of your technology. Factors related to customers will also be considered, including the business's brand reputation and image, breadth and diversity of the customer base, special relationships, forward integration, and the strength of your marketing and sales efforts. Finally, the strategy team will evaluate your current resource position, including relative cost position, capacity and distribution of resources, back integration, ability to acquire additional resources, and any special relationships with suppliers/stakeholders.

Unlike the Industry Attractiveness Analysis, in which you rated each factor based on your predictions for the future, the Competitive Position Analysis focuses on you and your competition *today*. Plot each industry participant separately on the Competitive Analysis chart. You may not need to evaluate each competitor for each variable, but include their positions for those variables that give them distinct competitive advan-

Analysis of Current Competitive Position					
	LEADER	**STRONG**	**FAIR**	**WEAK**	√
MARKET POSITION					
Market Share					
Market Participation					
Pricing Leadership					
PRODUCT POSITION					
Protected Position					
Differentiation					
Product Line/Service Breadth					
Technology					
CUSTOMER POSITION					
Brand Reputation/Image					
Breadth/Diversity Customer Base					
Special Customer Relationships					
Forward Integration					
Marketing/Sales					
RESOURCE POSITION					
Cost Position					
Resource Capacity & Distrib.					
Backward Integration					
Resource Acquisition Ability					
Special Supplier/Stakeholder Relationships					
OVERALL					

√ = **Key Factor affecting Competitive Position**

tages or disadvantages. Again, the summary rating chart is followed by definitions of each factor.

There are four basic positions one may hold relative to competition. The *Leader* position is just that: One is alone, the best in the industry, usually able to define what the industry is and to participate in all industry functions. The *Strong* are equal to the best of competition with no important deficiencies but are unable to surpass other strong competitors.

The *Fair* suffer major deficiencies, are usually unable to match all aspects of the industry definition, and find themselves lacking in certain competitive areas that may or may not be critical, depending on industry conditions. The *Weak* have significant flaws in their ability to compete and usually face extinction unless they correct those weaknesses. *Weak* competitors usually exist when there is no leadership in the industry and when the best competitors are *Fair* and have large deficiencies themselves.

Market Share. Describe the current distribution of market share in the industry. A *Leader* usually has twice the market share of the next largest competitor. *Strong* denotes share that is equal to the best in the industry and usually applies when share is fairly concentrated (25–30 percent blocks, as opposed to fragments of 10 percent or less). *Fair* applies to share that is viable or niched in a segment. It can also indicate a fragmented industry where participating competitors each hold 10 percent or less of the market. *Weak* denotes participation at insignificant levels and implies that the business is at the mercy of larger competitors.

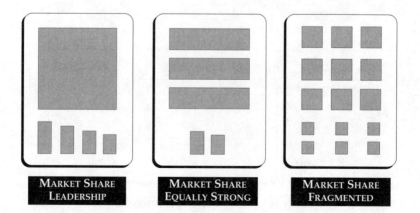

MARKET SHARE
LEADERSHIP

MARKET SHARE
EQUALLY STRONG

MARKET SHARE
FRAGMENTED

Market Participation. Evaluate the extent to which you and your competitors participate in all the markets described in the Industry Definition. A *Leader* would participate in all the industry's markets; a *Weak* competitor would be niched into a few or only one of the markets served by the industry.

Pricing Leadership. Assess industry participants' leadership in raising prices. Price reductions are aggressive and can be used by any participant at any time. The key is the ability to *raise* prices and the willingness of the rest of competition to follow.

A *Leader* can raise prices and make them stick. *Strong* denotes an ability to raise prices equal to the rest of competition, or the ability to lead at times and to follow on other occasions. *Fair* portrays an occasional role in pricing industry products/services, while *Weak* suggests no price leadership capability.

Protected Position. Evaluate the degree to which you and your competitors can claim patent, proprietary know-how, technical excellence, or franchise position of products/services. The *Leader* stands alone with capabilities that are extremely difficult to replicate. *Strong* is equal to the best, while *Fair* suggests major deficiencies. *Weak* describes a business that is vulnerable in all areas.

Product Line/Service Differentiation. Analyze the differentiation of products/services of each key industry participant. Although competitors may or may not provide the full product line/service coverage, they may be able to differentiate the line by quality, performance, or support services.

You can think of product line/service differentiation in terms of the unique advantages offered by a product or service. Consider both the number of advantages a product has and the size of those advantages.

A *Leader* has significantly the best degree of differentiation. *Strong* is equal to the best, while *Fair* is faced with deficiencies. *Weak* cannot meet the differentiation of the *Leader* or equally *Strong* competitors.

Product Line/Service Breadth. Assess the degree to which you and your competitors are capable of supplying the complete range of products/services described in the Industry Definition.

Leader represents the only competitor capable of a complete product and/or service array. *Strong* applies if two or more competitors participate fully, or if the best competitors are equally deficient in coverage. *Fair* reflects gaps in coverage, and *Weak* denotes serious deficiencies.

Technology. Assess the technological excellence of industry participants, a critical aspect of the quality and cost-effectiveness of the products/services you provide.

A *Leader* is alone in its ability to provide high-quality and cost-effective products. Again, *Strong* is equal to the best. *Fair* is significantly deficient, while *Weak* is vulnerable and cannot meet the standards of technology in the industry.

Brand Reputation/Image. Describe industry competitors' reputations as seen by customers, clients, and others in the industry. Advertising, historical reputation, and current events all shape a business's image.

A *Leader* stands alone and is heralded as such by both competitors and customers. When someone is asked who represents the industry, the *Leader* comes to mind first. *Strong* suggests a ranking equal to the best. *Fair* is mentioned as an afterthought, and people may need a reminder that a *Weak* competitor is even part of the industry.

Breadth/Diversity of Customer Base. Describe the customer base supplied by each key industry participant. The greater the number of customers and the more diverse their type and market participation, the better the competitive balance of the industry is likely to be, because competitors are less vulnerable to economic or market shifts in a particular segment. In industries that rely on repeat business, customer breadth and diversity are essential. In industries that tend to do business with a client occasionally or only once over many years, a vast potential customer base bodes well for the continued viability of the unit.

The *Leader* has superior coverage, supplying the widest array of customers as described in the Industry Definition. *Strong* is equal to the best; *Fair* participates with significant gaps in coverage, while *Weak* is deficient in several areas.

Special Customer Relationships. Evaluate the special relationships between industry participants and customers. Customer commitments contracted over extended periods of time and strong contacts or personal relationships with customers can provide a significant competitive advantage. Unique relationships with customers who have connections with other industries can also provide useful knowledge about related products and services.

The *Leader* has a superior array of relationships, *Strong* is equal to the best of the competition, *Fair* is significantly deficient compared to the *Leader* or *Strong* competitors, and *Weak* is not competitive in this category.

Forward Integration. Describe participants' abilities to move closer to the end-user of the industry's products/services. The line of crossing into another industry should be clearly delineated. Captive downstream use of an industry's products/services should be distinguished from the entry into another industry that uses the raw materials. For example, if a company that sells oxygen in small tanks for home use decides to begin selling walkers and other home medical products, they have not become more forward-integrated, they have entered a new industry.

A *Leader* in forward integration is alone in its ability to supply the end-use products, services, and/or functions of the industry. *Strong* is equal to the best; *Fair* is significantly lacking in forward integration and is somewhat dependent on others to represent its products/services. *Weak* is without forward integration as compared with competition and relies heavily or entirely on others in this area.

Marketing/Sales. Rate the marketing/sales expertise of those in the industry. Effective marketing and sales require accurate and clear portrayal of the business's products/services, sound feedback of customer needs and responses, and the ability to interpret others' strategies and tactics.

A *Leader* does this better than anyone else. *Strong* is equal to the best, *Fair* is deficient in important areas, and the *Weak* are unable to read customers' needs accurately or to portray their products effectively.

Cost Position. Describe the relative cost positions of industry participants, as defined by the total cost of the unit on a profit-and-loss basis (the operating cost of the enterprise). The ability to compete in any industry is dependent on cost position, although this factor is more critical in some industries than in others (e.g., commodities).

The *Leader* is the lowest-cost provider of industry products/services. *Strong* is equal to the best in the industry. *Fair* is a higher-cost operation, either because of important disadvantages or because volume is insufficient to cover the basic costs of invested assets (plant, people, administration, etc.). *Weak* denotes major cost disadvantages related to the provision of products/services.

Capacity and Distribution of Resources. Assess competitors' relative abilities to meet demand for products/services based on the available resources required, and evaluate the ability to maintain pace with the growth projections of the industry. Sufficient plant capacity, skilled personnel, distribution and service facilities, and marketing and sales coverage are all components of this evaluation.

A *Leader* can cover growth in demand significantly better than can its other competitors. *Strong* denotes equal coverage capability. *Fair* represents a fully stretched entity unable to absorb additional business volume. *Weak* applies to a unit having difficulty keeping up with current business.

Backward Integration. Assess the degree of backward integration, or how completely the businesses in the industry provide the raw materials and skills they need to create their products and services. As with forward integration, the line between entering another industry and having captive supply of raw materials must be clearly recognized.

The *Leader* has the most complete backward integration. *Strong* is equal to the best; *Fair* is deficient in significant aspects, while *Weak* is extremely vulnerable and dependent on others to provide the raw materials used for its products and services.

Resource Acquisition Ability. Analyze competitors' ability to acquire new resources required to meet growth. The acquisition of capital, skills, technical competence, production capacity, and marketing/sales coverage may be critical over the life of an industry.

A *Leader* has the unique ability to draw new resources at will. *Strong* is equal to the best in the industry. *Fair* would have difficulty acquiring new resources, and *Weak* is unable to renew or add resources without making large concessions.

Special Supplier/Stakeholder Relationships. Assess the competitive advantage resulting from contracting supply of raw materials at advantageous prices and from significant contacts or personal relationships with suppliers or other stakeholders. Unique relationships with suppliers in other industries that provide information about related products/services can also be beneficial.

The *Leader* has the best array of relationships, *Strong* is equal to the best of competition, *Fair* is significantly deficient compared to the *Leader* or *Strong* competitors, and *Weak* is unable to compete in this category.

Key Factors and Overall Rating. The Competitive Position Analysis determines what will be needed to compete successfully over the planning period. Several elements will usually be most important and will determine the overall rating of competitive position. The *Leader* is the best; the difference is so clear that other industry competitors and customers would agree. A *Strong* overall rating denotes a current position equal to the best of the competition and is often seen in a leaderless industry. *Fair* describes a position that is correctable, but only with serious cost and effort. *Weak* denotes a unit that should be considered for abandonment or total revision of its structure and character.

MATRIX OF INDUSTRY ATTRACTIVENESS AND COMPETITIVE POSITION

Now that the team has analyzed the industry's attractiveness and your competitive position, it may be useful to consider how those two assessments interact and what that suggests for your strategic direction. On the chart that follows, draw a vertical line representing the industry's potential as determined in the Industry Attractiveness Analysis. Indicate

COMP. POSITION	INDUSTRY ATTRACTIVENESS			
	EXCELLENT	GOOD	FAIR	POOR
LEADER				
STRONG				
FAIR				
WEAK				

the competitive positions of key industry participants on the line according to their overall ratings: *Leader, Strong, Fair,* or *Weak.*

The matrix reflects both the prospects for the industry and the current ranking of competition. The industry prospects and competitive positions are not written in stone, however, and should be viewed as a guide to provoke creative strategic solutions.

CHOOSING THE BUSINESS STRATEGIES

Now that you have analyzed your industry and your position in it, you are ready to begin the process of selecting the business strategies your business will pursue. Each case is different, and the "right" strategies are ones that capitalize on the industry opportunities and the business's strengths, while minimizing or managing external threats and internal weaknesses.

In our experience, strategies fall into four categories, or Strategic States (see Chapter 9). Matching the Strategic State to the business and

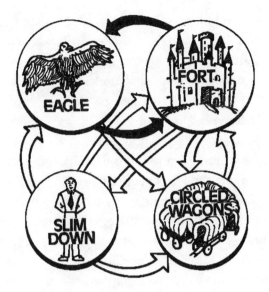

industry condition is critical. For example, a high-growth prospect supported by rapid change in technology and substantial increases in customer base would point to a time for *Eagles,* and the pursuit of new products and markets. It is generally best to pursue those opportunities with the use of a *Fort*'s plentiful and deployable resources.

On the other hand, the industry and business may have created a saturated market. Rapid growth can no longer be sustained, and high-cost marketing efforts will drain profits and damage industry profitability. Entering a *Slim Down* State may be natural, or a continued aggressive *Fort* strategy may be correct for the business as it capitalizes on other competitors' rationalizations and tries to gain leadership in the industry.

Then, there are industry prospects in which growth is moderate, the customer base is large and well established, market share is stable, and opportunities have narrowed to process improvements and methods efficiencies. Current conditions and prospects point to *Fort* strategies—the perfecting of what is at hand, excellence of operations, and maintenance of market share and position. There may be opportunities to take share away from fragmented competition or to take advantage of a *Leader*'s weak spot. While still in the *Fort* Strategic State, the time may be right to market-penetrate.

Each industry and business is faced with unique problems and opportunities; no formula can take those unique characteristics into account. The identification of a Strategic State and the selection of business strategies emerge naturally out of a careful examination of the strengths and weaknesses of the business and the opportunities and threats in its environment.

On the following pages, you'll find suggestions of business strategies that may be appropriate, given your business's position on the Matrix of Industry Attractiveness and Competitive Position.

Through discussion and examination of the previous evaluations, the planning team should identify the Strategic State that summarizes your intended strategies, and the business strategy options that would seem feasible to pursue. In some cases, one Strategic State will emerge as the only logical alternative at this point in the process. In other cases the Strategic State options will be narrowed to two or three, with accompanying packages of business strategies. Even if consensus around one Strategic State is achieved quickly, developing alternative cases can be useful for these reasons:

- A business can go in more than one direction naturally.
- Developing entirely different case(s) can be stimulating and revealing. In some situations, the alternative can become the prime case.
- Evaluating contingencies allows for fallback or recovery planning if events occur that hinder or halt the implementation of a strategic plan.
- Preparing the organization in advance for potential risks reduces surprises and accelerates the ability to deal with new developments.

Refer back to the Matrix of Industry Attractiveness and Competitive Position. Into which of the sixteen areas does your organization fall?

Your industry's potential for profitability and your competitive position in it will determine the kind of strategies that are likely to be successful at this time. For example, businesses falling into the areas circled on the next page are potential candidates for pursuing *Eagle* strategies (see Chapter 9 for a more detailed description of the *Eagle* Strategic State).

COMP. POSITION	INDUSTRY ATTRACTIVENESS			
	EXCELLENT	GOOD	FAIR	POOR
LEADER	◯	◯	◯	
STRONG	◯	◯		
FAIR	◯			
WEAK	◯			

EAGLE BUSINESS STRATEGIES

- *Initial market development:* Invest in creating a primary market demand for a brand new product; start a new business. This strategy often requires strong technical service and application engineering, a large expense budget, and adequate capitalization.

- *Develop new products for new markets:* Invest in developing, manufacturing, and marketing new products for new markets. Even though a loose relationship may exist between current products and the new products, an investment in new and unfamiliar areas is required. Remember that "new" in this case means new to the business that is embarking on the strategy, not necessarily new to the world.

- *Develop new products for existing markets:* Develop, broaden, or replace products in the present product line, selling into existing markets. These products are not line extensions of existing products using current technology; they are new in every sense to either the producer or the market. The new products may require entirely new technology and production capacity and extensive testing to gain customer approval.

- *Develop new markets for existing products:* Expand existing markets by geography or type for the existing product line. The new markets have applications for the products but have not used them before and will require extensive education, testing, or other assurances before use is approved. Markets may be domestic or foreign, but they do not have previous experience with your products.

- *Build excess capacity:* Build additional capacity (not incremental capacity) for existing products beyond current needs to meet anticipated growth. This is undertaken to fulfill ambitious projections (usually double-digit), or to permit expansion strategies relating to share. It may also be used to persuade customers that the reliability of supply is overwhelming, in order to reduce their concern about converting to products in this industry.

- *Develop a foreign business:* Establish a separate business in a foreign country in the same industry as the domestic business, but for a market with different characteristics. This usually results in increased sales volume and lowered receivables and inventory in the current business unit due to displacement of product.

- *Forward integration:* Bring in-house what were previously external functions or products that fall between the current business and the ultimate consumer. The goals are to increase sales and to lower production costs through more stable production schedules.

FORT BUSINESS STRATEGIES

If your organization is in either a *Leader* or a *Strong* position, regardless of industry prospects, you are probably a *Fort,* and *Fort* strategies will be natural for you to consider pursuing.

All *Fort* strategies have as their overall purpose one of these two goals:

COMP. POSITION	INDUSTRY ATTRACTIVENESS			
	EXCELLENT	GOOD	FAIR	POOR
LEADER	◯	◯	◯	◯
STRONG	◯	◯	◯	◯
FAIR				
WEAK				

- *Maintain market position* (same products/same markets): Maintain overall market share with the existing product line in existing markets; ensure continuing excellence in product line growth and differentiation and in the marketing and services required for growth and development.

or

- *Market penetration:* Increase market share by manipulating marketing mix (lower price, increase product and sales service, increase advertising). Market penetration is the equivalent of declaring war between nations, and the risks are high. The strategy may be initiated or used to respond to an attack by others. It pits one *Fort* against another and will require all the resources of each competitor until the strategic goals are achieved or the strategy is abandoned.

Within the parameters of those overall goals, the following *Fort* strategies can be pursued:

- *Export existing products:* Invest in marketing selected products of the domestic business to foreign markets, which may or may not have similar competitors and market dynamics; this involves the dedication of supply from domestic capacity to established positions in foreign markets. Product is committed to the export target markets in order fully to utilize capacity, to provide differentiated market participation, and to provide alternative outlets when domestic demand is low.

- *License:* License your products or processes to others to exploit the technology, patents, know-how, brand franchise, and so on, of the business. This option is high-risk, because controlling the use of the proprietary products and information can be difficult.

- *Backward integration:* Incorporate what were previously external support functions, operations, or products into the business. This is done to improve reliability of supply and/or consistency of raw material quality, to reduce costs, or to preempt competitors' own backward integrations.

- *Technological efficiencies:* Improve operating efficiency through technological improvements in physical plant, equipment, or processes. Probable benefits include decreased variable costs, increased fixed costs, and possibly increased profits.

- *Methods/functions efficiencies:* Invest in new ways of doing existing tasks by adding new "soft" technology (e.g., new patterns of work flow, computer-aided production planning, and inventory control) to improve effectiveness or efficiency. This can include steps like organizational restructuring or the application of computer technologies to customer service activities.

SLIM DOWN BUSINESS STRATEGIES

Businesses that are *Fair* relative to their competitors (or *Weak* in a *Good* industry) may be in need of a *Slim Down* Strategy.

- *Product line rationalization:* Narrow the product line to the most profitable products. Supplement or complement the product line with products purchased from other producers rather than continue in-house production.

COMP. POSITION	INDUSTRY ATTRACTIVENESS			
	EXCELLENT	GOOD	FAIR	POOR
LEADER				
STRONG				
FAIR		◯	◯	◯
WEAK		◯		

- *Production rationalization:* Further standardize design, components, and manufacturing processes; concentrate facilities; subcontract out elements of production (buy versus make).

- *Market rationalization:* Prune back the markets served by the business to the most profitable and/or higher-volume segments (including type of market or its geographical scope). Withdraw from certain market segments, or discontinue coverage to a function downstream within the market.

- *Distribution rationalization:* Prune back the distribution system to a more effective network. This may include cutting back to the highest-volume distributors or reshaping by geography or type (e.g., a reconfiguration using consolidated locations or elimination of warehouses or functions to achieve the same coverage as in the past).

- *Little jewel:* Strip down a business to the most profitable piece, and possibly reinvest proceeds of divestiture in the retained operation. A recovery in profitability justifies consideration of new or expansionist strategies.

CIRCLED WAGONS BUSINESS STRATEGIES

A business with a *Weak* competitive position may need to pursue the survival strategies of the *Circled Wagons* Strategic State. While the chart below indicates the positions of those businesses likely to be in this life-threatening condition, a business in *any* position may suddenly find itself in *Circled Wagons* because of a product safety crisis, an environmental disaster, or other major threats.

- *Traditional cost cutting; edict management:* Use management edicts to reduce costs uniformly; the short-term use of "dictatorial" management style involving budget cuts, layoffs, freezes on salary increases, hiring, and so forth.

- *Hesitation:* Slow down or establish moratoriums on new capital invest-

COMP. POSITION	INDUSTRY ATTRACTIVENESS			
	EXCELLENT	GOOD	FAIR	POOR
LEADER				
STRONG				
FAIR	◯			
WEAK	◯	◯	◯	◯

ment and new expenses because of capital limitations, dangers of overextending management, or market uncertainties. Hesitation does not prevent expenditures or new capital investment for normal maintenance of the business. The timing and duration of the strategy is critical.

- *Pure survival:* Maintain the business during extremely adverse conditions by eliminating functions and products or by underfinancing any activity. This strategy involves moratoriums on all expansions (expense capital, people, projects), and the radical divestiture or restructuring of assets, businesses, and people.

- *Unit abandonment:* Divest the business because it cannot remain viable or because it is more valuable to someone else. End participation in an industry via divestiture, shutdown of existing operations to incur book value writeoff, or the withdrawal of all capital financing, thereby allowing a business to wind down. This option may be appropriate when one or more of the following is present: zero or negative growth, obsolete plants and technology, exhausted management, negative income and negative cash flow, or enormous fixed investment required to improve competitive position (e.g., International Harvester's abandonment of farm machinery).

VISION AND STANDARDS OF EXCELLENCE

Out of detailed assessments of current and expected conditions, the strategy team agrees on an overall strategic direction for the business. When the direction and strategies are communicated to the organization, the team is essentially saying, "We believe these are the right things to do—the things that will help us to be successful in the future."

At this point in the process, and not before, we advocate that the team begin to craft a Vision of the future. The Vision describes what the organization needs to be and is capable of becoming by a specific year in the future. The Vision is not a pie-in-the-sky wish list, nor is it a description of an organization that is perfect in every way. It is a challenging but realistic picture of the business as it will be when the strategies have been fully implemented.

Placing the creation of the Vision at this point in the process is a departure from the conventional wisdom that advocates envisioning where you want to be and then finding ways to get there. While that seems logical, it ignores the fact that the future of any entity depends to a great extent on its past and present. What an organization is capable of achieving in a specific period of time can be very different from what it would like to achieve in an ideal world. Achieving the Vision depends on people's belief that it is possible. By creating a Vision before examining the present state of the business, a management team risks evoking the response: "You can't get there from here."

Creating a Vision with direct linkage to strategies communicates an achievable and unifying goal to all employees—one that is inspiring because it is both challenging and realistic.

In summary, a Vision:

- Describes the organization in the future when its strategies are realized and its Mission and core values are achieved
- Is a tool for communicating the results an organization expects over a specific time frame
- Becomes the context for organizational goal-setting (strategic projects and programs, annual plan and budgets, and functional action plans)

A Vision need not necessarily be conveyed to the organization or its customers in written form. However, it is useful to draft a written statement to ensure that the members of the planning team have a common understanding of the direction and goals.

Developing a Vision involves selecting a point in the future (i.e., five years from now) and, as a group with substantial input from others in the organization, describing what you want to be at that point. The Vision should be rich in visual detail and should be written in the present tense (as if you were speaking in the year you've selected). The Vision should describe who you are, what you do, what you believe, and how you work together.

A Vision answers these questions: At a selected point in the future,

- What will we do for a living?
- Where will we stand in relation to our competitors?

- How will our customers, suppliers, and employees see us?
- What will we stand for?

Process for Developing a Vision

- List topic areas to be covered in the Vision—e.g., business, customers, clients, suppliers, people, community, safety, environment, technology
- Brainstorm ideas—using brief statements
- Select and refine the critical few
- Review and select what will be included in Vision
- Shape Vision statement by refining and restating draft paragraphs
- Circulate draft Vision to key people throughout the organization for their input and revise accordingly

Using a Vision to Obtain Commitment

- Craft the message for clarity and simplicity
- Communicate the Vision to everyone frequently and in many different ways
- Ask for feedback and reality tests
- "Walk the talk"—make sure your actions are consistent with the Vision
- Achieving understanding and buy-in is hard work—never assume the job is easy or finished

STANDARDS OF EXCELLENCE

Getting "there" (to the state described in the Vision) from "here" (the current state of the business) will inevitably involve some changes in how work is done in the organization. There are a wide variety of paths to reach any goal, and choosing between them and establishing priorities can be difficult. This task can be simplified by breaking the Vision down into manageable pieces—the Standards of Excellence. These are much more specific than the Vision and involve measurable things the organization can and must do to ensure that the Vision becomes reality. This is a key part of the process, and one that is frequently overlooked.

The Standards of Excellence offer specific performance standards that will help the organization reach the Vision. In different Strategic States, the Standards of Excellence may describe very different conditions. Excellence in a growth environment is quite different from excellence when survival is the issue.

Standards of Excellence can be used to provide common goals for the entire organization, monitor progress and measure achievement, identify areas that require improvement, and set performance objectives.

In summary, Standards of Excellence:

- Can be observed, described, and measured
- Specify the conditions essential for the attainment of the Vision and the achievement of strategic goals
- Make the Vision unique and specific to your organization
- Specify what activities/outcomes will be recognized and rewarded by the organization
- Are written as performance objectives for the organization or for specific functions/departments
- Are used to track and monitor progress
- Are a tool for measuring current performance versus the ideal

Standards of Excellence describe specific measurable results in the areas that are most critical to the organization. These are some of the areas that may be included:

- Customers: number, mix, industry, type
- Products: number, mix, development of new products
- Performance: quality, efficiency, financial excellence
- People: hiring, development, core values
- Service: service quality, responsiveness, customer satisfaction
- Suppliers: partnerships, selection criteria, quality
- Requirements: legal, environmental, safety, financial

Examples of Standards

- Customers' orders are processed correctly, shipped on time and invoiced without error 99% of the time.

- Our business performs consistently better on_____financial measure year to year than any competitor.

Process for Developing Standards

- Consider each sentence in the Vision separately.
- Brainstorm possible standards: What would we as an organization be doing if we had attained this part of the Vision?
- If possible, divide into small groups. Each group will be responsible for refining standards in a certain area. The group answers the question: "How might we be able to measure the results of this activity?"
  —financial measures
  —surveys of customer and employee satisfaction
  —tracking number of requests, proposals, contracts, turnover, etc.
- Seek input on the draft of the Standards of Excellence from people in the organization. This is a key part of the process, because people will be responsible for meeting these standards. Their input can help ensure that the standards are true measures of success. In addition, people are more likely to commit to achieving those goals if they have input into their creation.

GAP ANALYSIS

Once you have outlined the standards that will be used to measure progress toward your Vision, the next step is for the team to rate your current performance on each standard. Use the following scale:

1. We never meet this standard
2. We rarely meet this standard
3. We sometimes meet this standard
4. We usually meet this standard
5. We always meet this standard

Surveys of customers, suppliers, and employees can provide more detailed and objective evaluations of progress toward key standards.

Using the same scale, identify where you would like to be in one year for each standard. While you would ideally like to see a "5" rating on each standard, try to assess realistically how much progress can be made and set priorities for those areas that will make the most difference in achieving your Vision.

The differences between the current and desired performance ratings will show you where the biggest "gaps" are occurring and may help you identify the most important standards for immediate attention. It will be critical for people throughout the organization to understand which standards have the highest immediate priority and why.

Standards	Name of Each Group Member								

At this point, the strategy team, with substantial input from the rest of the organization, has done much of the up-front work of strategic planning. While that is a necessary and integral part of the process, it is only that—part of the process.

Without careful and energetic implementation, the most carefully crafted plans will sit on the shelf. The vital next step is to translate the Standards of Excellence into a clear delineation of key strategies and strategic projects and programs.

PLANNING IMPLEMENTATION

Planning for the implementation of the chosen strategic projects and programs produces benefits at three levels. At the individual level, planning provides a clear picture of the work and how it will be executed. At the group level, planning encourages communication, increases the commitment to group goals, and clarifies individual responsibilities. At the organizational level, the plan becomes the basis for coordination and resolution of conflicts between groups.

Planning implementation, however, is more than the development of a plan of action. It includes the following steps to ensure the plan will be successfully carried out:

- *Clarifying the purpose:* Making sure that the desired outcome of change is clear, legitimate, widely understood, and shared. The need for change has to exceed the resistance to change
- *Ensuring commitment:* Making sure that there is a commitment from a strong network to make the change work, that the right people are willing to invest in the change, and that it gets management's attention
- *Strategic projects:* Selecting projects and developing action plans to achieve the purpose and make the organizational changes required for success
- *Monitoring progress:* Making sure that progress is real, that benchmarks are set and realized, and that indicators are established to ensure progress is made

CLARIFYING THE PURPOSE

You have already developed an overall Vision for the organization. For major strategic projects and programs, it is useful to define a clear, challenging statement of purpose as well. This purpose specifies the desired outcome of the strategic project articulated in both emotional (visual, enticing) and pragmatic (quantitative) ways.

Questions to ask:

- Has a purpose been articulated?
—What's in it for customers?
—What's in it for employees?
- Is the statement of purpose understandable?
- Is the purpose shared by others in the organization?
- Is the purpose energizing?

Typical problems encountered:

- No single statement of purpose; everyone has his or her own version
- No link with customers; the purpose focuses too much on what we want, not what the customer wants
- The statement of purpose is too complex to be easily understood and translated into practice

ENSURING COMMITMENT

The goal is to establish a coalition of relevant and committed individuals who agree with the change effort and visibly support it.

Questions to ask:

- Have we identified the key individuals who must support this change for it to be successful?
- Do we have buy-in for the change to happen?
- Have champions/sponsors been identified?

Actions required:

- Identify key players who must be involved
- Identify what's in it for them to participate in the change effort
- Form a coalition of key players who will be advocates and sponsors
- Leverage sponsors to create a network of support

- Anticipate who will resist and manage the network in order to moderate the resistance

Typical problems encountered:

- No political buy-in
- Not sharing the glory of the success
- Assuming that a technical solution is sufficient (e.g., I have the right answer, why isn't everyone else smart enough to see it?)

DEFINING STRATEGIC PROJECTS

The selection and definition of strategic projects involves answering the following questions:

1. What are we trying to solve? (What is broken? What needs to improve and by how much?)
2. What will things operate/feel like when the problems are solved? (What does success look like?)
3. What measures and data will we use to demonstrate that progress has been made toward solving the problems? (How do we know we have improved?)
4. What problems, issues, units, functions, etc., are we consciously including and excluding from our projects? (What is our scope?)
5. What is our problem statement or project title, given the above? (What do we tell people we are really going to do?)

MONITORING PROGRESS

Monitoring progress ensures that the results of the change effort are tracked and widely shared.

Questions to ask:

- Have desired results been articulated in concrete terms?
- Have milestones been set along the way?
- Are results tied to business goals?
- Will outcomes of the change be evident to customers?
- Are specific individuals accountable for results?

Actions required:

- Develop measures of progress for change effort
- Track progress
- Share credit for achieving results widely
- Hold people accountable for results

Typical problems encountered:

- No measures of success, so no indicators of progress
- Not tying change effort to business results
- People want results too soon and judge the effort prematurely
- We assume that one change only affects one initiative; we miss the unanticipated consequences of change

STRATEGIC PROJECT FRAME

A Strategic Project Frame is the primary tool for managing and controlling the work and is also issued to review and appraise the project. We call it a frame because it provides the initial boundaries for the work on the project (although this, too, must allow room for strategies to evolve). It contains the following:

- Project title/name
- Project scope/timing
- Project standards/mileposts/results
- Resource requirements: equipment, people, money or other resources needed to complete the action steps

Complete a Strategic Project Frame for each key project or program. If the project team has been assembled, they should be initially involved in the framing of the project.

Strategic Project Frame

Project Title/Name	
Project Scope/Timing	
Project Standards, Mileposts, Results	
Key Obstacles to Overcome	
Resource Requirements	

APPENDIX C

Developing New Skills

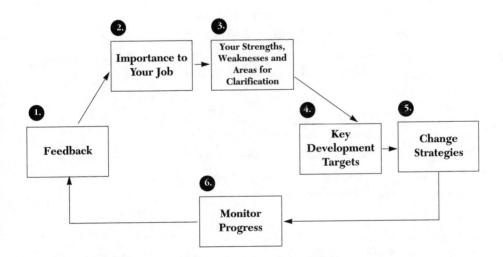

There are six steps in the process of developing new skills:

1. Get feedback on your current skills and behaviors. The brief questionnaires in Appendix A can be a good starting point.
2. Decide which skills are most important for your current job and for jobs you aspire to do in the future.

3. Outline your current strengths, weaknesses, and any areas that need further clarification.
4. Identify key development targets—in which areas would you like to improve?
5. Decide which change strategies you will choose to help you improve in the areas you've identified.
6. Determine how you will monitor progress on your development goals.

This appendix will outline the various change strategies that may be available to you.

CHANGE STRATEGIES FOR DEVELOPING NEW SKILLS

There are five major approaches for developing or improving your skills:

1. *Reading*
2. *Self-monitoring:* Establish a tracking system to determine if you are making progress toward your objectives.
3. *Coaching/Consulting/Mentoring:* Identify someone who is qualified and willing to provide instruction and guidance in the areas you want to improve.
4. *Training:* Attend a formal course, workshop, or seminar that includes training in the areas you want to improve.
5. *Job Assignments:* Find a way to enhance your current job (special projects, new challenges) or change assignments to provide yourself with developmental experiences.

1. READING

There are hundreds of books, journals, magazines, and newspapers related to the field of strategy and leadership. The notes section at the end of this book is a good place to start. It is also important to keep in mind the value of reading that is not directly related to business but is useful for providing a fresh perspective. Biographies of world leaders are particularly useful for understanding strategic thinking. Science fiction has inspired people to think creatively and to innovate.

2. SELF-MONITORING

This approach is one you can do by yourself. First, decide which skill you want to concentrate on. It is best to select a skill that is very relevant for your job, but that you do not use very much. The behaviors most suited to self-monitoring are consulting, recognizing, and monitoring.

Using the Self-Monitoring Checklist, list examples of the skill or behavior. Refer to the relevant sections of this book for examples. You will note that the form shows the days of the week in columns. The checklist is good for a period of six weeks. Either during the day or at the end of the day, make a checkmark when you use one of the behaviors. Set a personal goal to use each example at least once per week, when appropriate. At the end of each week, review your performance and determine how well you did.

After a period of six weeks, you will find that you are beginning to use the new skills and behaviors more naturally, without the need to plan on using them consciously. When that happens, you can switch to another area needing improvement and use the same process. If it is not too confusing, you can use self-monitoring for more than one area at a time. However, it is most effective to work on no more than three new skills and behaviors simultaneously.

3. COACHING/COUNSELING/MENTORING

Not all new skills lend themselves to improvement by self-monitoring. If you are unsure how to use a skill well, or aren't sure if you're improving, you may want to find a coach or mentor to help. Coaching is most appropriate for a skill that you are already using with mixed success. In other words, you are doing it, but not as effectively as you would like. You need someone to observe you and provide feedback about what you are doing well and what you are doing poorly. A competent coach will provide advice on how to use the skill more effectively and, if necessary, demonstrate or model the behavior for you.

The first step is to identify someone who is qualified to provide coaching and likely to take the time and effort to help you. Some good possibilities to consider include your boss, a trusted colleague, or a training specialist in your organization.

SELF-MONITORING CHECKLIST

Skill or Behavior: _____

	Week 1					Week 2					Week 3					Week 4					Week 5					Week 6				
Behavior Example	M	T	W	Th	F	M	T	W	Th	F	M	T	W	Th	F	M	T	W	Th	F	M	T	W	Th	F	M	T	W	Th	F

Next, determine how you will approach this person and try to persuade him/her to help you. Finally, you should identify an appropriate
setting and time for the coaching to take place, and you should consider
if any special resources are needed or if cooperation is needed from
other people in addition to the coach.

4. TRAINING

You may find that there is nobody available who has both the skill and
the time to provide appropriate coaching. Formal training is an alternative approach for improving your use of a new skill. Formal training is
especially appropriate for learning complex skills that may not be easily
acquired through occasional coaching. Training is useful for learning
conceptual and analytical skills, such as those required for planning
and problem-solving. It is also appropriate for learning complex inter-
personal skills, such as those involved in influencing. Classroom learning works best when it is tied to your real needs on the job.

There are many workshops and courses available for such practices
as planning, problem-solving, clarifying, consulting, delegating, inspiring, mentoring, and team-building. However, for some areas it may be
more difficult to find an appropriate training opportunity.

Once you have identified an area you would like to improve with formal training, the next step is to identify an appropriate training opportunity. You should conduct a search of available training courses,
including those within your own organization, those in nearby colleges
and universities, those offered by professional associations, and those
offered by consulting companies. In selecting an appropriate training
opportunity, it is important to probe beneath the superficial description
presented in a catalog description or training brochure to determine
whether the needed skills are indeed taught in a particular course or
workshop. For example, you may ask the trainer or sales representative
to explain how a course or workshop will improve your skills in a specific area, and you should determine if you will actually have the opportunity to practice the skills during the course.

Once you have determined that the training is important and have registered for a course, don't be tempted to pull out at the last minute because of real or imagined conflicts.

5. THE JOB

Research has shown that the most effective tool for training and development is the job itself. The job as classroom provides challenge, which in turn provides an opportunity for learning through experience. In a study conducted by the Center for Creative Leadership, executives reported that nearly half of the events that made a lasting impact on their ability to manage were job assignments. Both new jobs and current jobs with intentionally constructed challenges are critical for continual learning, growth, and change.

The Center's research indicates that these kinds of jobs provide valuable experience:

- Scope Assignments include a huge leap in responsibility, moving into an unfamiliar line of business, and/or being switched to a line management position from a staff job.
- Scratch Assignments include building something from nothing and taking action under uncertainty. These jobs challenge you to consult with others, make quick decisions, and surround yourself with talented people.
- Fix-it Assignments include positions where an organization is in trouble and things need to be turned around.
- Project/Task Force Assignments are short-term and highly visible and often require people to work in areas where they have little content knowledge. Such jobs provide a test of your decision-making, communication, and ability to establish strong relationships.
- A Line-to-Staff Assignment provides people with an opportunity to move from a line position to a job in such areas as planning, finance, and administration. People often need to learn new technical skills on the job. This kind of change can also help you appreciate the importance of influencing others over whom you have no direct authority.
- Demotions, Missed Promotions, and Unchallenging Jobs are just that. There is a mismatch between person and job, due to a crisis,

poor performance, or unrealized aspirations. Above all, these moves teach humility and give people an opportunity to persevere and clarify their own goals and values.

For more information on selecting job challenges to build new skills, see *The Lessons of Experience* by Morgan W. McCall, Jr., Michael H. Lombardo, and Ann M. Morrison (Lexington, MA: Lexington Books, 1988).

OUTLINING CONCRETE DEVELOPMENT STRATEGIES

Using the following worksheet, list one area you've chosen to focus your development on. Identify:

Area for Development: _____

1. **Developmental Goal:**_____

2a. **Typical Strategy:**   b. **Actions/Next Steps:**

_____   _____

                                       _____

                                       _____

3a. **Additional Strategies:**   b. **Actions/Next Steps:**

_____   _____

                                       _____

                                       _____

_____   _____

                                       _____

                                       _____

1. Your specific development goal (behaviors you will change to enhance current and future effectiveness).
2. a. The strategy you would typically choose to work towards this goal. (Refer to the change strategies. Are you normally a "reader"? Someone who seeks coaching?)
   b. For this strategy, list the specific actions you will take to achieve your goal.
3. a. Two additional strategies you will use as supplements. (If you are typically a reader, what other strategy will you pursue?)
   b. For each of these additional strategies, list the specific actions you will take to achieve your goal.

MONITORING YOUR PROGRESS

As with any type of action planning, monitoring your progress requires you to set milestones and identify resources.

Here are some tools people use to monitor change:

- Keep your development plan in your in-box or mail folder; consult it frequently.
- Contract with your boss and co-workers. Describe to them the change you want to make, and ask them to give you ongoing feedback.
- Use family members as sources of feedback.
- Use calendar or project planning software to remind yourself of your commitment to change and the actions you've laid out for yourself.
- Use the self-monitoring checklist.
- Choose a trusted colleague and ask for help.

NOTES

Chapter 1. Strategy: Myths, Misconceptions, and Wrongheaded Notions

1. *Business Week,* May 16, 1994, p. 8.
2. H. Edward Wrapp, "Good Managers Don't Make Policy Decisions," in *The Strategy Process: Concepts and Contexts,* ed. Henry Mintzberg and James Brian Quinn (Englewood Cliffs, N.J.: Prentice Hall, 1992), p. 35.
3. Kenneth R. Andrews, *The Concept of Corporate Strategy* (Homewood Ill.: Irwin, 1987), p. xi.
4. A.D. Chandler, *Strategy and Structure* (Cambridge: MIT Press, 1962), p. 13.
5. Tim Hindle, *Field Guide to Strategy* (Boston: Harvard Business/The Economist, 1994), p. 3.
6. Robert G. Eccles and Nitin Nohria, *Beyond the Hype: Rediscovering the Essence of Management* (Boston: Harvard Business School Press, 1992), p. 87.
7. "The Vision Thing," *Forbes,* August 30, 1993, p. 43.
8. "In the News," *Executive Directions,* April 1994, p. 6.
9. Henry Mintzberg, *The Rise and Fall of Strategic Planning* (New York: Free Press, 1994), p. 243.
10. See Leonard R. Sayles, *The Working Leader* (New York: Free Press, 1993), pp. 130–53.
11. Peter Vaill, "Strategic Planning for Managers," article prepared for inclusion in a book of readings published by NTL Institute, Arlington, Va., 1982.
12. Donald C. Hambrick and Phyllis A. Mason, "Upper Echelons: The Organization as a Reflection of Its Top Managers," *Academy of Management Review,* 9, no. 2 (1984):193–206.

13. Adapted from Charles M. Hampden-Turner, "Dilemmas of Strategic Learning Loops," in *Strategic Thinking: Leadership and the Management of Change,* ed. John Hendry, Gerry Johnson, and Julia Newton (Chichester, UK: John Wiley & Sons, 1993), pp. 327–45.

Chapter 2. Beyond the Boardroom: Why Strategy Is Everyone's Business

1. Deborah Shapley, *Promise and Power: The Life and Times of Robert McNamara* (Boston: Little, Brown, 1993), p. 67.
2. Ralph E. Winter, "Spending on Research and Development in U.S. to Rise 3% to $182 Billion in '95," *Wall Street Journal,* January 9, 1995, p. B7A.
3. "Managing By Values," *Business Week,* August 1, 1994, p. 47.
4. *Business Week,* February 18, 1967, p. 202.
5. Harry Levinson, "Why the Behemoths Fell: Psychological Roots of Corporate Failure," *American Psychologist,* May, 1994, pp. 428–35.
6. *New York Times,* September 23, 1992.
7. Dyan Machan, "Starting Over," *Forbes,* July 4, 1994, p. 53.
8. Thomas A. Stewart, "Your Company's Most Valuable Asset: Intellectual Capital," *Fortune,* October 3, 1994, p 68.
9. Quoted in Julia Vitullo-Martin and J. Robert Moskin, *The Executive's Book of Quotations* (New York: Oxford University Press, 1994), p. 25.
10. Theodore Levitt, *Thinking about Management* (New York: Free Press, 1991), p. 19.
11. Stephanie K. Marrus, *Building the Strategic Plan* (New York: John Wiley & Sons, 1984), p. 9.
12. Frederick Rose, "Job-Cutting Medicine Fails to Remedy Productivity Ills at Many Companies," *Wall Street Journal,* June 7, 1994, p. A5.
13. David Kirkpatrick, "Groupware Goes Boom," *Fortune,* December 27, 1993, p. 100.
14. John A. Byrne, "Belt-tightening the Smart Way," *Business Week,* Enterprise Special Issue, 1993, p. 34.
15. Donna Brown Hogarty, "IBM Research Goes Back to Basics," *Management Review,* December, 1993, p. 23.

Chapter 3. Dilemmas in Strategy-making: Damned If You Do . . .

1. *Webster's Seventh New Collegiate Dictionary* (Springfield, MA: G. & C. Merriam Company, 1972), p. 233.
2. Charles Hampden-Turner and Charles Baden Fuller, *Working Paper No. 51,* Centre for Business Strategy, London Business School, 1989.

3. Leonard Sayles, opening remarks, Center for Creative Leadership Conference, "New Demands for Leadership: Responding to Turbulence," January 6, 1994.

4. Hampden-Turner and Fuller, *Working Paper No. 51.*

5. *Alan Deutschman, "How H-P Continues to Grow and Grow,"* Fortune, May 2, 1994, pp. 90–100.

6. Quoted in *Fortune*, August 22, 1994, p. 20.

7. Charles Hampden-Turner and Alfons Trompenaars, *The Seven Cultures of Capitalism* (New York: Currency Doubleday, 1993), p. 9.

8. Carter Henderson, *Winners: The Successful Strategies Entrepreneurs Use to Build New Businesses* (New York: Holt, 1985), pp. 190–91.

9. Robert Howard, "The CEO as Organizational Architect," *Harvard Business Review*, September—October 1992, p. 112.

10. Robert G. Eccles and Nitin Nohria, *Beyond The Hype: Rediscovering the Essence of Management* (Boston: Harvard Business School Press, 1992).

11. Patrick Oster, "How a New Boss Got ConAgra Cooking Again," *Business Week*, July 25, 1994, p. 73.

12. Richard Brandt, "Bill Gates's Vision," *Business Week*, June 24, 1994, p. 57.

13. John H. Sheridan, "A CEO's Perspective on Innovation," *Industry Week*, December 19, 1994, p. 11.

Chapter 4. Empowerment with Teeth: Getting People Involved in the Formal Strategy Process

1. Richard B. Freeman and Joel Rogers, *Worker Representation and Participation Survey, Report on the Findings*, Princeton Research Associates, 1994, p. iii.

2. Henry Mintzberg, *The Rise and Fall of Strategic Planning*, (New York: Free Press, 1994).

3. Gary Hamel and C. K. Prahalad, *Competing for the Future* (Boston: Harvard Business School Press, 1994).

4. Marshall Loeb, "How to Grow a New Product Every Day," *Fortune*, November 14, 1994, p. 269.

5. Gail E. Schares, "Percy Barnevik's Global Crusade," *Business Week*, Enterprise Special Issue, 1993, p. 208.

6. Shawn Tully, "Why to Go for Stretch Targets," *Fortune*, November 14, 1994, pp. 145–58.

7. "Inside the Empire of Exxon the Unloved," *The Economist*, March 5, 1994, p. 69.

8. Quoted by Dave Beal in *St. Paul Pioneer Press*, February 7, 1994.

9. Susan E. Peterson, "NSP Shaking Up Its Corporate Culture," *Minneapolis Star and Tribune,* January 18, 1993.

10. James M. Kouzes and Barry Posner, *The Leadership Challenge* (San Francisco: Jossey-Bass, 1987).

11. Saul W. Gellerman, *Motivation in the Real World* (New York: Dutton, 1992).

12. William B. Moffett, "Outcomes of Teamwork at FMC," *At Work, Stories of Tomorrow's Workplace,* March/April 1994, p. 9.

13. Anonymous quote from preconference comments, Center for Creative Leadership Conference, "New Demands for Leadership," January 5–7, 1994.

Chapter 5. Structured Improvisation: Planning for Strategies to Emerge

1. Andy Warhol in *Observer,* March 1, 1987. Cited in Julia Vitollo-Martin and J. Robert Moskin, eds., *The Executive's Book of Quotations* (New York: Oxford University Press, 1994), p. 24.

2. William G. Lee, "A Conversation with Herb Kelleher," *Organizational Dynamics,* Autumn 1994, p. 70.

3. *Ibid.*

4. Brian Dumaine, "The Bureaucracy Busters," *Fortune,* June 17, 1991, p. 50.

5. Anonymous quote from preconference comments, Center for Creative Leadership Conference, "New Demands for Leadership," January 5–7, 1994.

6. Lynne Joy McFarland, Larry E. Senn, John R. Childress, *21st Century Leadership* (Los Angeles: Leadership Press, 1993), p. 76.

7. John A. Byrne, "Enterprise," *Business Week,* Enterprise Special Issue, 1993, p. 14.

8. Polly LaBarre, "The Dis-Organization of Oticon," *Industry Week,* July 18, 1994, p. 26.

9. Amar Bhide, "Hustle as Strategy," *Harvard Business Review,* September–October 1986.

Chapter 6. The Role of the Front-line Strategist

1. B. C. Forbes in *Forbes,* January 2, 1995, p, 300.

2. Irimajiri speech, April 7, 1987, quoted in Paul Ingrassia and Joseph B. White, *Comeback: The Fall and Rise of the Automobile Industry* (New York: Simon & Schuster, 1994), p. 439.

3. "The Crunch at Chrysler," *The Economist,* November 12, 1994, p. 93.

4. Cited in *The Pryor Report,* 10;5A, p. 6.

5. Ronald Henkoff, "Finding, Training and Keeping the Best Service Workers," *Fortune,* October 3, 1994, p. 116.

6. *Ibid.*

7. Gary Yukl, *Leadership in Organizations* (Englewood Cliffs, N.J.: Prentice-Hall, 1994), p. 109.

8. Marshall Loeb, "How to Grow a New Product Every Day," *Fortune,* November 14, 1994, p. 269.

9. "OAW Guide Is a Profile of High-Performance Companies," *Work in America,* September, 1994, pp. 3–5.

Chapter 7. The Strategy Integrator: The Role of the "Manager"

1. F. Scott Fitzgerald, *The Crack-Up* (1936), quoted in Julia Vitullo-Martin and J. Robert Moskin, eds., *The Executive's Book of Quotations* (New York: Oxford University Press, 1994), p. 145.

2. James Autry, *Life and Work: A Manager's Search for Meaning* (New York: William Morrow, 1994).

3. Eugene F. Bryan, letter to the editor, *New York Times,* July 17, 1994, p. F11.

4. David Kirkpatrick, "Could AT&T Rule the World?" *Fortune,* May 17, 1993, p. 57.

5. Robert Howard, "The CEO as Organizational Architect: An Interview with Xerox's Paul Allaire," *Harvard Business Review,* September–October 1992, p. 113.

6. Jean B. Keffeler, "Managing Changing Organizations," *Vital Speeches of the Day,* 58 (November 15, 1991): 92–96.

7. Quoted in Brian Burrough, *Vendetta: American Express and the Smearing of Edmond Safra* (New York: HarperCollins, 1992).

8. Thomas A. Stewart, "How To Lead a Revolution," *Fortune,* November 28, 1994, p. 60.

9. Stephen Kerr, "On the Folly of Rewarding A While Hoping for B," *Academy of Management Journal,* 18 (1975): 769–83.

10. Brian Dumaine, "Who Needs a Boss," *Fortune,* May 7, 1990.

11. "Work Week," *The Wall Street Journal,* December 13, 1994, p. A1.

12. Princeton Research Associates, *Worker Representation and Participation Survey: Report on the Findings,* December, 1994, p. 13.

13. Richard Freeman and Joel Rogers, *Worker Representation and Participation Survey: First Report of Findings,* December 5, 1994, p. 6.

14. Warren Bennis, *On Becoming a Leader* (Reading, Mass.: Addison-Wesley, 1989), p. 45.

15. Tom Peters, *Liberation Management: Necessary Disorganization for the Nanosecond Nineties* (New York: Fawcett Columbine, 1992), p. 102.

16. Lawrence M. Miller, quoted in Joy Lynne McFarland, Larry E. Senn, and John R. Childress, *21st Century Leadership: Dialogues with 100 Top Leaders* (New York: Leadership Press, 1993).

17. James Autry, *Life and Work: A Manager's Search for Meaning* (New York: William Morrow, 1994).

18. Gary Yukl, Stephen Wall, and Richard Lepsinger, "Preliminary Report on the Validation of the Managerial Practices Survey," in K. E. Clark and M. B. Clark, eds., *Measures of Leadership* (West Orange, N.J.: Leadership Library of America, 1990), pp. 223–38.

Chapter 8. The Strategic Leader: The Role of the Senior Executive

1. Quoted in William Safire and Leonard Safir, eds., *Leadership* (New York: Simon & Schuster, 1990), p. 76.

2. Len Sayles, Opening Remarks, "New Demands for Leadership: Responding to Turbulence," Center for Creative Leadership Conference, January 6, 1994.

3. Peter Vaill, "Strategic Planning for Managers," Article prepared for inclusion in a book of readings published by NTL Institute, Arlington, Va., 1982.

4. Letter to the Editor, *Harvard Business Review*, January–February 1995, p. 142.

5. James O'Toole and Warren Bennis, "Our Federalist Future: The Leadership Imperative," *California Management Review*, Summer 1992, p. 87. Emphasis in original.

6. Quoted in *Fortune*, May 16, 1994, p. 18.

7. Donna Shalala, quoted in Joy Lynne Mc Farland, Larry E. Senn, and John R. Childress, *21st Century Leadership* (New York: Leadership Press, 1993), p. 97.

8. Theodore Hesburgh, quoted in Safire and Safir, *Leadership*, p. 240.

9. Hedrick L. Smith, quoted in Mc Farland, Senn, and Childress, *21st Century Leadership*, p. 99.

10. William B. Moffett, "Outcomes of Teamwork at FMC Corporation," *At Work: Stories of Tomorrow's Workplace*, March/April 1994, p. 10.

11. Shawn Tully, "Why Go for Stretch Targets?" *Fortune*, November 14, 1994, p. 145.

12. Robert G. Eccles and Nitin Nohria, *Beyond the Hype: Rediscovering the Essence of Management* (Boston: Harvard Business School Press, 1992), p. 10.

13. Quoted in John H. Sheridan, "Lew Platt: Creating a Culture for Innovation," *Industry Week*, December 19, 1994, p. 26.
14. Quoted in Christopher A. Bartlett and Sumatra Ghoshal, "Changing the Role of Top Management: Beyond Strategy to Purpose," *Harvard Business Review*, November-December 1994, p. 84.
15. Quoted in *Ibid.*
16. Quoted in Sheridan, "Lew Platt," p. 28.
17. James A. Autry, *Life & Work: A Manager's Search for Meaning* (New York: William Morrow, 1994).
18. Donald C. Hambrick, "The Top Management Team: Key to Strategic Success," *California Management Review*, vol. 30, no. 1 (1987).
19. Richard C. Hodgson, Daniel J. Levinson and Abraham Zaleznik, "The Executive Role Constellation: An Analysis of Personality and Role Relations in Management," Harvard University Division of Research, Graduate School of Business Administration, Boston, 1965.
20. Arthur Radford, 1957, quoted in a book of quotations.
21. Kurt Lewin, "Frontiers in Group Dynamics," *Human Relations* 1:5–41.
22. Quoted in Michael L. Lovdahl and David H. Gaylin, "Commentary: Strategy Communication," Temple, Barker & Sloane, Inc., Lexington, Mass.
23. "Varian, Palo Alto, California," *Industry Week*, October 17, 1994, p. 47.
24. Anonymous pre-meeting quotes, Center for Creative Leadership Conference, "New Demands for Leadership: Responding to Turbulence," January 5–7, 1994.

Chapter 9. How to Think Like a Strategist

1. Quoted in William Safire and Leonard Safir, eds., *Leadership* (New York: Simon & Schuster, 1990), p. 41.
2. William D. Jockle of Manus was instrumental in helping us understand the principles of strategy and in developing the Strategic States model. We thank him.
3. "A Global Science Machine," *International Business*, January 1995, p. 54.
4. Quoted in G. Pascal Zachary, "How 'Barbarian' Style of Phillipe Kahn Led Borland into Jeopardy," *Wall Street Journal*, June 2, 1994, p. A6.
5. "A Third Front in the Cola Wars," *Business Week*, December 12, 1994, p. 67.
6. Gail DeGeorge, "Someone Woke the Elephants," *Business Week*, April 4, 1994, p. 52.
7. Rahul Jacob, "Corporate Reputations," *Fortune*, March 6, 1995, p. 60.

8. Alan Deutschman, "How H-P Continues to Grow and Grow," *Business Week,* May 2, 1994, p. 90.

9. Ronald Henkoff, "Getting Beyond Downsizing," *Fortune,* January 10, 1994, p. 58.

10. Jennifer W. Martineau and Walter W. Tornow, *Issues and Observations,* (complete issue), 14, no. 3 (Center for Creative Leadership, 1994):8.

11. "He's Gutsy, Brilliant, and Carries an Ax," *Business Week,* May 9, 1994, p. 63.

12. *Business Week,* November 7, 1994, p. 6.

13. Brian Dumaine, "The Trouble with Teams," *Fortune,* September 5, 1994, p. 87.

14. John A. Byrne, "Belt-tightening the Smart Way," *Business Week,* Enterprise Special Issue, 1993, p. 38.

Chapter 10. Getting It Done: How to Gain Support for Your Strategic Initiatives

1. Quoted in William Safire and Leonard Safir, *Leadership* (New York: Simon & Schuster, 1990), p. 22.

2. Phillipe August Villiers, quoted in Thomas Bonoma, *The Marketing Edge: Making Strategy Work* (New York: Free Press, 1985).

3. Peter M. Senge, *The Fifth Discipline* (New York: Doubleday Currency, 1990).

4. Quoted in Safire and Safir, *Leadership,* p. 175.

INDEX